OHIO RULES OF EVIDENCE HANDBOOK

with Common Objections & Evidentiary Foundations

2026

(Rules last amended in 2025)

Provides free access to
BarkaiBots
interactive AI courtroom simulations that function both as
responsive practice partners and built-in coaches.
Using a computer, tablet, or phone,
users rehearse advocacy skills and receive immediate coaching 24/7
when conducting simulations with AI witnesses, judges, and
opposing counsel

John Barkai

Colors on the cover are from the Ohio state flag

2026 Changes: this book includes free access to BarkaiBots— interactive AI courtroom simulations that function both as responsive practice partners and built-in personal coaches.

Using a free ChatGPT account on a desktop, laptop, phone, or tablet, lawyers and law students can rehearse advocacy skills 24/7 by conducting realistic simulations with witnesses, judges, and opposing counsel. During practice, BarkaiBots respond in real time like courtroom participants; after the exercise, they provide immediate, personalized feedback and coaching to help users refine their advocacy.

These simulations allow users to practice direct and cross-examinations, handle evasive witnesses, make and respond to objections, lay evidentiary foundations, conduct impeachment, present openings and closings, argue motions, and run full mock trials.

Users may also customize a BarkaiBot by uploading a short hypothetical fact pattern, allowing practice with scenarios drawn from their own cases while avoiding disclosure of confidential client information. BarkaiBots allow advocates to rehearse, receive coaching, and refine their advocacy before stepping into the courtroom.

ACCESS IS ON PAGE A-84

Regarding copyright – there is none.
Formatting. There is no standard formatting style for presenting rules of evidence. This handbook uses formatting intended to make the understanding and application of the rules as clear as possible - but clarity and ease of understanding of the rules of evidence by using the text alone is almost impossible.
Disclaimer: The author is not offering legal advice. Your trial judge may view the law and foundations differently. The law is whatever the judge in your case says it is. Any errors in this book are mine.

Corrections, omissions, suggestions?
See any or have some? Contact me at barkai@hawaii.edu

Common Citation Forms: Evid.R. xxx or even ORE xxx.

Recent Amendments:
Rule 615 in 2025 (deleting the word "alleged" when it modifies "victim.")
Rules 101 and 702 in 2024.
Rule 101, 601, 607, 609, and 616 in 2023.
Rules 404(b), 502, 606(B), 801(C) & (D)(1), and 803(16) in 2022.

Ohio Rules of Evidence Handbook
with Common Objections & Evidentiary Foundations

Professor John Barkai
William S. Richardson School of Law
University of Hawaii
Honolulu, HI 96822
March 2026

ISBN: 9798680076170

INTRODUCTION
This handbook of the Ohio Rules of Evidence Handbook was designed to be brought to court and be at your side in the office.

Besides the rules of evidence, the **"added value"** in this handbook is the following sections:

A) **Making and Responding to Common Objections** (16 pages)
 - **a discussion of the most common objections**
 - **a list of the most common objections**

B) **Evidentiary Foundations and Impeachment** (over 60 pages)
 - **25 examples of the most common evidentiary foundations**
 - **a brief discussion of differing standards for authenticating digital evidence** (such as email, text messages, social media sites, internet sites)

C) **Free Access to BarkaiBots - 24/7 interactive AI courtroom simulations that function both as responsive practice partners and built-in coaches to help users improve their advocacy.**

The sample foundation and impeachment questions are "bare-bones" foundations which include the minimum questions and answers necessary to get testimony or exhibits admitted into evidence

Professor John Barkai

SUMMARY OF CONTENTS

Introduction iii
Summary of Contents iv
Expanded Table of Contents v
Sample Pages from Deeper in the Handbook viii
Ohio Rules of Evidence (by number and title) xiii
Most Commonly Used Hearsay Sub-Sections xv
Ohio Rules of Evidence (full rules) 1-37

Appendix

Making and Responding to Common Objections .... A - 1
    A List of Common Objections A-16
Evidentiary Foundations A-17
    Evidentiary Foundations Index A-18
    Sample Foundational Questions (Predicates) A-35
    Digital Evidence – Electronically Stored Information – ESI. A-62
History and Restyling of the Federal Rules of Evidence A-78
Teaching Evidence since 4 B.C. A-79
Books by John Barkai A-80
Dedication & About the Author A-82
BarkaiBots: 24/7 Oral Practice Tools for Trial Advocacy .. A-83
Access to BarkaiBots A-84

Expanded Table of Contents

Introduction iii
Summary of Contents... iv
Expanded Table of Contents v
Sample Pages from Deeper in The Handbook viii
Ohio Rules of Evidence (by number and title) xviii
Most Commonly Used Hearsay Sub-Sections xx
Ohio Rules of Evidence (full rules)... 1-37

Appendix
Making and Responding to Common Objections....................... A-1
Why Do Lawyers Object?... A-1
Make an Objection in Four Steps... A-2
How to Respond to an Objection A-2
If You are a Judge Who Has to Rule on the Objection A-3
Multiple Lawyers and Multiple Clients A-3
Judges Apply the Rules of Evidence More Loosely in Nonjury Trials. .. A-3
The Key to Objection is Rule 103 .... A-3
Important Points about Rule 103.. A-4
Rule 103. Rulings on Evidence A-4
Objections - Rules - Constitutional Issues A-5
Motions in Limine A-5
Phrases that Suggest Inadmissible Information A-6
Inadequate Objections A-6
Offers of Proof A-6
Nonjury Trials – Seldom Reversed A-7
Common Phrases from Court Opinions A-7
Common Objections to the Form of the Question A-8
    Argumentative (Harassing, Badgering) A-8
    Asked and Answered A-8
    Assuming Facts Not in Evidence... A-9
    Beyond the Scope A-9
    Compound Question. A-10
    Cumulative A-10
    Lack of Foundation A-10
    Leading Question A-11
    Motion to strike A-11
    Narrative Question A-12
    Non-Responsive Answer A-12
    Speculation.. A-13
    Vague and Ambiguous Question A-13
Golden Rule A-13
Speaking Objections... A-14
Coaching the Witness... A-14
Relevance A-14
A Few Useful Definitions A-15
    Stipulation A-15
    Offer of Proof.. A-15
    Motion in Limine A-15
    Limited Admissibility A-15
    Intrinsic Impeachment A-15
    Extrinsic A-15
    Collateral A-15
A List of Common Objections A-16

Evidentiary Foundations A-17
Foundations – Laying the Foundation - Predicates A-17
Evidentiary Foundations Index A-18
Bare-Bones Foundations A-20
Admissibility v. Weight A-21
Example of Admissibility and Weight A-21
3 Simple Questions A-22
Steps for Introducing Exhibits A-23
The Common Evidentiary Foundations A-25
The Phrases to Move Evidence into a Trial A-26
Useful Points to Remember A-27
    Into Evidence A-27
    Make an Offer of Proof A-27
    Hearsay Within Hearsay A-27
    Public Records Do Not Have to Be Open to The Public A-27
    Compute Generated Record Is Not Hearsay A-27
    Emails Offered to Show Notice, Knowledge or Fear Are Not Hearsay ... A-27
    Demonstrative Evidence A-27
    Chain of Custody A-27
    Distinctive Characteristics A-27
    Authenticate with Personal Knowledge and Distinctive Characteristics A-28
    Affidavits Are Hearsay and Inadmissible at Trial A-28
    Harrowing A-28
    OTP – Offered to Prove A-28
    Rules Do Not Explain How to Introduce Evidence in Court A-28
    Laying A Foundation Is Like A Sport A-28
    Mark, Show, Approach, Foundational Questions, Offer A-28
    Magic Words A-29
    Speak in Generic Terms A-29
    Publish Means to Show Them Now A-29
    Chain of Custody Is Only for Fungible Items or Samples to Test A-29
    Basic Tasks A Trial Lawyer Should Be Able to Do A-29
    Best Evidentiary Foundation Resources A-29
Important Evidence Rules to Guide You A-30
    R 103, 104, 901, 612, 613. 801, 803(6), 901, 902(11), 902(13&14), 105, 106, 1006
Opponent Has the Burden on The Issue of Trustworthiness A-31
Basic Foundation & Impeachment Examples A-32
    Nita Liquor Commission Facts A-33
    Officer Bier's Report A-34
    Diagram of Cut-Rate Liquor Store Area A-35
    Photograph of A Scene A-36
    Diagram of The Scene A-37
    Real Evidence – Thunderbird Wine Bottle A-38
    Offering A Contract into Evidence A-39

Refreshing Memory – Anything A-40
Writing Used to Refresh Memory – R612 .... A-42
Refreshing Memory with A Leading Question A-43
Recorded Recollection (Author's Rule) A-44
Business Records - Custodian of Records – R803(6) A-46
Business Records Are KRAP A-47
Self-Authenticating Business Records Form - Texas A-48
Demonstrative Evidence - Similar to The Real Item A-49
Impeachment - Prior Written Inconsistent Statement A-50
Impeachment by Omission A-52
Impeachment by Inconsistent Oral Deposition A-54
Impeachment - Inconsistent Oral Deposition - Short Form A-55
Impeachment - Inconsistent Oral Deposition - Long Form A-56
Impeachment - Inconsistent Oral Statement A-57
Learned Treatises Use on Direct Exam – R803(18) A-58
3 Key Points for Using Learned Treatises A-59
Learned Treatises: Use on Cross A-60
Voicemail and Phone Conversations A-61

Digital Evidence – Electronically Stored Information – ESI A-63
    A Variety of Different Standards A-63
    Distinctive Characteristics and Circumstantial Evidence A-65
    Presenting Digital Evidence from A Cell Phone in Court A-66
    Digital Evidence and Self-Authentication A-67
Digital Evidence Foundations A-63
    Email – Outgoing A-68
    Email – Incoming A-69
    Text Message – Received by Witness A-70
    Social Media: Facebook, Instagram, Snapchat, Twitter A-71
    Internet Website – Web Posting A-72
    Fax – Incoming A-73
Foundation for Expert Opinion A-74
History and Restyling of the Federal Rules of Evidence A-78
Teaching Evidence since 4 B.C. A-79
Books by John Barkai A-80
Dedication & About the Author A-82
BarkaiBots: 24/7 Oral Practice Tools for Trial Advocacy A-83
Access to BarkaiBots A-84

SAMPLE PAGE FROM DEEPER IN THE HANDBOOK

Make an Objection in Four Steps
1) Stand up.
2) Say, "Objection ____" (Fill in the blank with your reason).
3) Identify your specific objection.
    a) At a minimum, say the topic type
        (Hearsay, Relevance, Improper Impeachment, Improper Character, Lack of Foundation, Leading Question, etc.)
    b) State the evidence rule number if you know it (404, 608, etc.).
    c) A combination of the above
        ("Objection, Improper Impeachment, R613")
4) Stop talking and listen to the judge.
Be prepared to state reasons for your objection and to make an argument to support your position.

How to Respond to An Objection?
1) Speak to the judge, not the lawyer who objected.
2) Explain to the judge why your evidence should be admissible. ("Your Honor, that statement is not hearsay because I am not offering it for the truth but rather to show notice.")
3) If you recognize that you did not lay an appropriate foundation for the evidence explain that you will do that. ("Your Honor, I will lay the foundation.")
4) If you recognize that the opposing counsel was objecting to the form of your question, which most often happens on your direct examination, simply say, "I'll rephrase." Rephrase the question and move on with your witness examination. Do not get sidetracked by the opposing counsel who might have objected just to throw you off track.
5) For any physical piece of evidence, statement, or testimony that you will be introducing, prepare in advance and have a reason why you believe that evidence is admissible. Be ready to make that argument to the judge.
6) If the objection is to relevance, and you think you will be able to show that it is relevant, say to the judge "I will connect it up in a few questions Your Honor." Such a statement is equivalent of saying "trust me." If you do that, you'd better connect it up or the judge will not trust you in the future.

SAMPLE PAGE FROM DEEPER IN THE HANDBOOK

A List of Common Possible Objections

Ambiguous	Improper opinion
Argumentative	Improper rehabilitation
Asked and answered	Inadmissible opinion
Assumes facts not in evidence	Incompetent witness
Authentication	Incomplete Inflammatory
Badgering	Insufficient foundation
Best evidence	Irrelevant (Relevance)
Beyond the scope	Lack of foundation
Bias	Lack of personal knowledge
Bolstering	Leading question
Calls for a conclusion	Misleading
Calls for speculation	Misquotes a witness or exhibit
Chain of custody	Misquotes evidence
Collateral	Misstates witness
Competence	More prejudicial than probative
Compound question	Motion to strike
Compromise / Settlement offer	Narrative
Confrontation (lack of)	(Question calls for a narrative)
Confusing	Narrative answer
Counsel is testifying	Non-responsive
Cumulative	Nothing pending
Document speaks for itself	Outside the scope of cross
Expert (Improper opinion)	Overly broad or general
Expert (not qualified)	Parole evidence rule
Habit	Personal knowledge
Harassing the witness	Prejudice (unfair)
Hearsay	Privilege communication
Hypothetical question misused	Relevance
Improper character evidence	Speculation/ Opinion/ Lack of personal knowledge
Improper characterization	Unintelligible
Improper impeachment	Vague

There are many more possible objections,
limited only by the lawyer's imagination.

Judges and the local legal culture in your jurisdiction may have other rules or approaches to objections that are not touched on in this handbook. Ask around and learn about them.

SAMPLE PAGE FROM DEEPER IN THE HANDBOOK

Steps for Introducing Exhibits

> **Preliminary steps are:**
> 1) **Have the exhibit marked for identification**
> 2) **Show the proposed exhibit to opposing counsel**
> 3) **Ask permission to approach the witness with the proposed exhibit**

1. **History - How the witness knows the exhibit.**
   Offer some testimony that the witness <u>knows</u> or is <u>familiar with</u> the evidence – such as a document, physical item, photo, diagram, scene, text message, email - or recalls the statement. Even if the witness has only seen the exhibit once before or has just been to the scene shown in the photograph once before, <u>once is enough</u>.

2. **The Litany (a ritualistic repetition of foundational questions)**
   a) Ask the court clerk to **mark the item** (using numbers or letters). The clerk will decide which system to use. In more serious cases in the jurisdiction's higher courts (typically where jury trials are allowed), exhibits are usually required to be marked at least before trial starts, and often during pretrial conferences.
   b) **Show opposing counsel** (this will prevent interruptions) and say, "Let the record reflect that I am showing the defense what has been marked as plaintiff's proposed exhibit number one."
   c) Ask the judge for **permission to approach** the witness. "May I approach the witness?"
   - **Q:** "**I show you what has been marked as** Plaintiff's (Prosecution's) (Defense's) proposed exhibit # x (or exhibit #x for identification purposes) **and ask whether you can identify it**" (You expect a "yes" answer here.)
   - **Q:** "**What is it?**" (They describe it in general terms. "It is the contract/photo of the scene/weapon recovered/drugs seized/diagram of the area/etc.")
   - **Q:** "**How do you know that?**" (They answer – "I recognize it. It has my signature on it. / I have been there many times before. / I put my initials on it and the defendant's name/etc.")

SAMPLE PAGE FROM DEEPER IN THE HANDBOOK

3. Show Condition or Comparison or Accuracy

Some comparison must be made between the exhibit in court and when the witness became familiar with the exhibit out-of-court. Of the examples that follow, only one such question is necessary.

- "Is this in the **same** condition as when you... [first saw it...seized it...etc.]?"
- "Is this in the **same or substantially** the same condition.... as when you…" (for item or document)
- "Is it a **fair and accurate representation** of the ... **as it was that day**?" (for diagram or pictures)
- "**Has it changed** in any significant way?"
- "**How does it compare** to the item you saw that day?"

4. Move or Offer the Exhibit into Evidence

"Your honor, **I offer the exhibit into evidence**." - or, "I move the exhibit into evidence."

You could instead say, "I offer proposed exhibit # 1 into evidence as exhibit # 1," but why make it so confusing? Just say, "I offer the exhibit into evidence."

The judge <u>might</u> ask the opposing counsel, "Any objections?" but the opponent should object immediately after the proponent offers the exhibit if there is an objection to the admissibility (not the weight). The judge should allow "voir dire" (immediate cross examination limited to the foundation and the admissibility) by the opponent of the exhibit.

SAMPLE PAGE FROM DEEPER IN THE HANDBOOK

Authentication of Text Message – An Example

Text Message
Received by Witness

Do you know Y?

Do you communicate with Y on a regular basis?

In what ways to you communicate with Y?

Did you receive a text message from the Y [recently; on or about _ date, on the topic of …, etc.]?

Would you recognize a printout of the message if you were to see it again?

Let me show you what has been marked as proposed exhibit # 1. Do you recognize it?

What is it? [Ans: A screenshot from my cell phone]

How do you know that this is a message from Y? [It is similar to other messages I have received from Y in that …]

How did it appear when it arrived on your phone? [Showed up under the name and with the picture I had previously assigned to Y]

What other distinctive characteristics did you notice about the message? [provide as many as distinctive characteristics possible]

Is it a fair and accurate representation of the text message you received [recently; on or about _ date, on the topic of visiting your son, etc.]?

Has it been altered in any way?

I would like to enter the proposed exhibit into evidence

OHIO RULES OF EVIDENCE

(Rules last amended 2025)

ARTICLE I. GENERAL PROVISIONS

Rule 101 Scope of Rules: Applicability; Privileges; Exceptions 1
Rule 102 Purpose and Construction; Supplementary Principles................1
Rule 103 Rulings of Evidence...2
Rule 104 Preliminary Questions 3
Rule 105 Limited Admissibility 3
Rule 106 Remainder of or Related Writings or Recorded Statements 3

ARTICLE II. JUDICIAL NOTICE

Rule 201 Judicial Notice of Adjudicative Facts 4

ARTICLE III. PRESUMPTIONS IN CIVIL AND CRIMINAL ACTIONS.

Rule 301 Presumptions in General in Civil Actions and Proceedings...........4
Rule 302 [Reserved} 4

ARTICLE IV. RELEVANCY AND ITS LIMITS

Rule 401 Definition of "Relevant Evidence" 5
Rule 402 Relevant Evidence Generally Admissible; Irrelevant Evidence Inadmissible...5
Rule 403 Exclusion of Relevant Evidence on Grounds of Prejudice, Confusion, or Undue Delay..5
Rule 404 Character Evidence not Admissible to Prove Conduct; Exceptions; Other Crimes, Wrongs, or Acts..6
Rule 405 Methods of Proving Character 7
Rule 406 Habit; Routine Practice 7
Rule 407 Subsequent Remedial Measures 7
Rule 408 Compromise and Offers to Compromise 7
Rule 409 Payment of Medical and Similar Expenses 8
Rule 410 Inadmissibility of Pleas, Offers of Pleas, and Related Statements..8
Rule 411 Liability Insurance 8

ARTICLE V. PRIVILEGES

Rule 501 General Rule 9
Rule 502 Attorney-Client Privilege and Work Product; Limitations on Waiver.....10

ARTICLE VI. WITNESSES
Rule 601 General Rule of Competency 11
Rule 602 Lack of Personal Knowledge 12
Rule 603 Oath or Affirmation 13
Rule 604 Interpreters 13
Rule 605 Competency of Judge as Witness 13
Rule 606 Competency of Juror as Witness 13
Rule 607 Impeachment 14
Rule 608 Evidence of Character and Conduct of Witness 14
Rule 609 Impeachment by Evidence of Conviction of Crime 15
Rule 610 Religious Beliefs or Opinions 16
Rule 611 Mode and Order of Interrogation and Presentation 16
Rule 612 Writing Used to Refresh Memory 17
Rule 613 Impeachment by Self-Contradiction 18
Rule 614 Calling and Interrogation of Witnesses by Court 18
Rule 615 Separation and Exclusion of Witnesses 19
Rule 616 Methods of impeachment 19

ARTICLE VII. OPINIONS AND EXPERT TESTIMONY
Rule 701 Opinion Testimony by Lay Witnesses 20
Rule 702 Testimony by Experts 20
Rule 703 Bases of Opinion Testimony by Experts 20
Rule 704 Opinion on Ultimate Issue 20
Rule 705 Disclosure of Facts or Data Underlying Expert Opinion 20

ARTICLE VIII. HEARSAY
Rule 801 Definitions 21
Rule 802 Hearsay Rule 22
Rule 803 Hearsay Exceptions; Availability of Declarant Immaterial 23
Rule 804 Hearsay Exceptions; Declarant Unavailable 26
Rule 805 Hearsay Within Hearsay 28
Rule 806 Attacking and Supporting Credibility of Declarant 28
Rule 807 Hearsay Exceptions; Child Statements in Abuse Cases 29

ARTICLE IX. AUTHENTICATION AND IDENTIFICATION
Rule 901 Requirement of Authentication or Identification 30
Rule 902 Self-Authentication 32
Rule 903 Subscribing Witness' Testimony Unnecessary 34

ARTICLE IX. CONTENTS OF WRITINGS, RECORDINGS, AND PHOTOGRAPHS
Rule 1001 Definitions 35
Rule 1002 Requirement of Original 35
Rule 1003 Admissibility of Duplicates 35
Rule 1004 Admissibility of Other Evidence of Contents 36
Rule 1005 Public Records 36
Rule 1006 Summaries 36
Rule 1007 Testimony or Written Admission of Party 36
Rule 1008 Functions of Court and Jury 37

ARTICLE XI. MISCELLANEOUS RULES
Rule 1101 [Reserved] 37
Rule 1102 Effective Date 37
Rule 1103 Title 37

THE MOST COMMONLY USED OHIO HEARSAY SUB-SECTIONS

Rule 801. Definitions 21
   (D) Statements Which Are Not Hearsay................................21
      (1) Prior Statement by Witness.......................................21
         (a) inconsistent statement - under oath
            (trial, hearing, or deposition) 21
         (b) consistent – offered to rebut 21
         (c) (prior identification) 21
      (2) Admission by Party-Opponent 21
Rule 802. Hearsay Rule 22
Rule 803. Hearsay Exceptions – Availability Immaterial 22
   (1) Present Sense Impression. 22
   (2) Excited Utterance 22
   (3) Then Existing Mental, Emotional, Or Physical Condition..........22
   (4) Statements for Purposes of Medical Diagnosis or Treatment 22
   (5) Recorded Recollection...23
   (6) Records of Regularly Conducted Activity (business records) 23
   (8) Public Records and Reports...23
   (17) Market Reports, Commercial Publications.................25
   (18) Learned Treatises...25
Rule 804. Exceptions 26
   (A) Definition of Unavailability. 26
      (1) Former Testimony 27
      (2) Statement Under Belief of Impending Death 27
      (3) Statement Against Interest 27
Rule 805. Hearsay Within Hearsay 28

OHIO RULES OF EVIDENCE
(with amendments through July 1, 2021)

ART. I. GENERAL PROVISIONS

Rule 101. Scope of Rules: Applicability; Privileges; Exceptions

(A) Applicability. These rules govern proceedings in the courts of this state, subject to the exceptions stated in division (D) of this rule.

(B) Privileges. The rule with respect to privileges applies at all stages of all actions, cases, and proceedings conducted under these rules.

(C) Definitions. As used in these rules:

(1) "Present" means the physical or remote presence of an individual.

(2) "Remote presence" means the presence of a person who is using live two-way video and audio technology.

(D) Exceptions. These rules (other than with respect to privileges) do not apply in the following situations:

(1) Determinations prerequisite to rulings on the admissibility of evidence when the issue is to be determined by the court under Evid.R. 104.

(2) Proceedings before grand juries.

(3) Proceedings for extradition or rendition of fugitives; sentencing; granting or revoking probation; proceedings with respect to community control sanctions; issuance of warrants for arrest, criminal summonses and search warrants; and proceedings with respect to release on bail or otherwise.

(4) Contempt proceedings in which the court may act summarily.

(5) Proceedings for those mandatory arbitrations of civil cases authorized by the rules of superintendence and governed by local rules of court.

(6) Proceedings in which other rules prescribed by the Supreme Court govern matters relating to evidence.

(7) Special statutory proceedings of a non-adversary nature in which these rules would by their nature be clearly inapplicable.

(8) Proceedings in the small claims division of a county or municipal court.

Rule 102. Purpose and Construction

The purpose of these rules is to provide procedures for the adjudication of causes to the end that the truth may be ascertained and proceedings justly determined. The principles of the common law of Ohio shall supplement the provisions of these rules, and the rules shall be construed to state the principles of the common law of Ohio unless the rule clearly indicates that a change is intended. These rules shall not supersede substantive statutory provisions.

Rule 103. Rulings on Evidence

(A) Effect of Erroneous Ruling. Error may not be predicated upon a ruling which admits or excludes evidence unless a <u>substantial right</u> of the party is affected; and

    (1) Objection. In case the ruling is one <u>admitting</u> evidence, a timely objection or motion to strike appears of record, stating the <u>specific ground</u> of objection, if the specific ground was not apparent from the context; or

    (2) Offer of Proof. In case the ruling is one <u>excluding</u> evidence, the <u>substance of the evidence was made known</u> to the court by offer or was apparent from the context within which questions were asked. Offer of proof is not necessary if evidence is excluded during cross-examination.

Once the court rules definitely on the record, either before or at trial, a party <u>need not renew</u> an objection or offer of proof to preserve a claim of error for appeal.

(B) Record of Offer and Ruling. At the time of making the ruling, the court may add any other or further statement which shows the character of the evidence, the form in which it was offered, the objection made, and the ruling thereon. It may direct the making of an offer in question and answer form.

(C) Hearing of Jury. In jury cases, proceedings shall be conducted, to the extent practicable, so as to prevent inadmissible evidence from being suggested to the jury by any means, such as making statements or offers of proof or asking questions in the hearing of the jury.

(D) Plain Error. Nothing in this rule precludes taking notice of plain errors affecting substantial rights although they were not brought to the attention of the court.

Rule 104. Preliminary Questions

(A) Questions of Admissibility Generally. Preliminary questions concerning the qualification of a person to be a witness, the existence of a privilege, or the admissibility of evidence shall be determined by the court, subject to the provisions of subdivision (B). In making its determination it is <u>not bound by the rules of evidence except</u> those with respect to <u>privileges</u>.

(B) Relevancy Conditioned on Fact. When the relevancy of evidence depends upon the fulfillment of a condition of fact, the court shall admit it upon, or subject to, the introduction of evidence <u>sufficient to support a finding of the fulfillment of the condition</u>.

(C) Hearing of Jury. Hearings on the admissibility of confessions shall in all cases be conducted out of the hearing of the jury. Hearings on other preliminary matters shall also be conducted out of the hearing of the jury when the interests of justice require.

(D) Testimony by Accused. The accused does not, by testifying upon a preliminary matter, become subject to cross-examination as to other issues in the case.

(E) Weight and Credibility. This rule does not limit the right of a party to introduce before the jury evidence relevant to weight or credibility.

Rule 105. Limited Admissibility

When evidence which is admissible as to one party or for one purpose but not admissible as to another party or for another purpose is admitted, the court, upon request of a party, shall restrict the evidence to its proper scope and instruct the jury accordingly.

Rule 106. Remainder of or Related Writings or Recorded Statements

When a writing or recorded statement or part thereof is introduced by a party, an adverse party may require the introduction at that time of any other part or any other writing or recorded statement which is otherwise admissible and which ought in fairness to be considered <u>contemporaneously</u> with it.

ART. II. JUDICIAL NOTICE

Rule 201. Judicial Notice of Adjudicative Facts
(A) Scope of Rule. This rule governs only judicial notice of adjudicative facts; i.e., the facts of the case.
(B) Kinds of Facts. A judicially noticed fact must be one not subject to reasonable dispute in that it is either (1) generally known within the territorial jurisdiction of the trial court or (2) capable of accurate and ready determination by resort to sources whose accuracy cannot reasonably be questioned.
(C) When Discretionary. A court may take judicial notice, whether requested or not.
(D) When Mandatory. A court shall take judicial notice if requested by a party and supplied with the necessary information.
(E) Opportunity to Be Heard. A party is entitled upon timely request to an opportunity to be heard as to the propriety of taking judicial notice and the tenor of the matter noticed. In the absence of prior notification, the request may be made after judicial notice has been taken.
(F) Time of Taking Notice. Judicial notice may be taken at any stage of the proceeding.
(G) Instructing Jury. In a civil action or proceeding, the court shall instruct the jury to accept as conclusive any fact judicially noticed. In a criminal case, the court shall instruct the jury that it may, but is not required to, accept as conclusive any fact judicially noticed.

ART. III PRESUMPTIONS

Rule 301. Presumptions in General in Civil Actions and Proceedings
In all civil actions and proceedings not otherwise provided for by statute enacted by the General Assembly or by these rules, a presumption imposes on the party against whom it is directed the burden of going forward with evidence to rebut or meet the presumption, but does not shift to such party the burden of proof in the sense of the risk of non-persuasion, which remains throughout the trial upon the party on whom it was originally cast.

Rule 302. [Reserved]

ART. IV. RELEVANCY AND ITS LIMITS

Rule 401. Definition of "Relevant Evidence"
"Relevant evidence" means evidence having any tendency to make the existence of any fact that is of consequence to the determination of the action more probable or less probable than it would be without the evidence.

Rule 402. Relevant Evidence Generally Admissible; Irrelevant Evidence Inadmissible
All relevant evidence is admissible, except as otherwise provided by the Constitution of the United States, by the Constitution of the State of Ohio, by statute enacted by the General Assembly not in conflict with a rule of the Supreme Court of Ohio, by these rules, or by other rules prescribed by the Supreme Court of Ohio. Evidence which is not relevant is not admissible.

Rule 403. Exclusion of Relevant Evidence on Grounds of Prejudice, Confusion, Or Undue Delay
(A) Exclusion Mandatory. Although relevant, evidence is not admissible if its probative value is substantially outweighed by the danger of unfair prejudice, of confusion of the issues, or of misleading the jury.
(B) Exclusion Discretionary. Although relevant, evidence may be excluded if its probative value is substantially outweighed by considerations of undue delay, or needless presentation of cumulative evidence.

Rule 404. Character Evidence Not Admissible to Prove Conduct; Exceptions; Other Crimes, Wrongs, or Acts

(A) Character Evidence Generally. Evidence of a person's character or a trait of character is not admissible for the purpose of proving action in conformity therewith on a particular occasion, subject to the following exceptions:

(1) **Character of Accused.** Evidence of a pertinent trait of character offered by an accused, or by the prosecution to rebut the same is admissible; however, in prosecutions for rape, gross sexual imposition, and prostitution, the exceptions provided by statute enacted by the General Assembly are applicable.

(2) **Character of Victim.** Evidence of a pertinent trait of character of the victim of the crime offered by an accused, or by the prosecution to rebut the same, or evidence of a character trait of peacefulness of the victim offered by the prosecution in a homicide case to rebut evidence that the victim was the first aggressor is admissible; however, in prosecutions for rape, gross sexual imposition, and prostitution, the exceptions provided by statute enacted by the General Assembly are applicable.

(3) **Character of Witness.** Evidence of the character of a witness on the issue of credibility is admissible as provided in Rules 607, 608, and 609.

(B) Other Crimes, Wrongs or Acts.

(1) **Prohibited uses**. Evidence of any other crime, wrong, or act is not admissible to prove a person's character in order to show that on a particular occasion the person acted in accordance with the character.

(2) **Permitted uses; notice**. This evidence may be admissible for another purpose, such as proving motive, opportunity, intent, preparation, plan, knowledge, identity, absence of mistake, or lack of accident. The proponent of evidence to be offered under this rule shall:

(a) provide reasonable notice of any such evidence the proponent intends to introduce at trial so that an opposing party may have a fair opportunity to meet it;

(b) articulate in the notice the permitted purpose for which the proponent intends to offer the evidence, and the reasoning that supports the purpose; and

(c) do so in writing in advance of trial, or in any form during trial if the court, for good cause, excuses lack of pretrial notice

Rule 405. Methods of Proving Character

(A) Reputation or Opinion. In all cases in which evidence of character or a trait of character of a person is admissible, proof may be made by testimony as to <u>reputation</u> or by testimony in the form of an <u>opinion</u>. <u>On cross</u>-examination, inquiry is allowable into relevant <u>specific instances of conduct</u>.

(B) Specific Instances of Conduct. In cases in which character or a trait of character of a person is an <u>essential element of a charge, claim, or defense,</u> proof may also be made of <u>specific instances</u> of his conduct.

Rule 406. Habit; Routine Practice

Evidence of the <u>habit of a person</u> or of the <u>routine practice of an organization</u>, whether corroborated or not and regardless of the presence of eyewitnesses, is relevant to prove that the conduct of the person or organization on a particular occasion was in conformity with the habit or routine practice.

Rule 407. Subsequent Remedial Measures

When, after an injury or harm allegedly caused by an event, measures are taken which, if taken previously, would have made the injury or harm less likely to occur, evidence of the subsequent measures is <u>not admissible to prove negligence or culpable conduct</u> in connection with the event. This rule does <u>not</u> require the <u>exclusion</u> of evidence of subsequent measures when offered for another purpose, such as proving <u>ownership, control, or feasibility of precautionary measures, if controverted, or</u> **impeachment**.

Rule 408. Compromise and Offers to Compromise

Evidence of (1) furnishing or offering or promising to furnish, or (2) accepting or offering or promising to accept, a valuable consideration in compromising or attempting to compromise a claim which was disputed as to either validity or amount, is not admissible to prove liability for or invalidity of the claim or its amount. Evidence of conduct or <u>statements</u> made in compromise negotiations is <u>likewise not admissible</u>. This rule does not require the exclusion of any evidence otherwise discoverable merely because it is presented in the course of compromise negotiations. This rule also does <u>not</u> require exclusion when the evidence is <u>offered for another purpose,</u> such as proving <u>bias or prejudice</u> of a witness, negativing a contention of undue delay, or proving an effort to obstruct a criminal investigation or prosecution.

Rule 409. Payment of Medical and Similar Expenses

Evidence of furnishing or offering or promising to pay medical, hospital, or similar expenses occasioned by an injury is not admissible to prove liability for the injury.

Rule 410. Inadmissibility of Pleas, Offers of Pleas, And Related Statements

(A) Except as provided in division (B) of this rule, evidence of the following is not admissible in any civil or criminal proceeding against the defendant who made the plea or who was a participant personally or through counsel in the plea discussions:

    (1) a plea of guilty that later was withdrawn;
    (2) a plea of no contest or the equivalent plea from another jurisdiction;
    (3) a plea of guilty in a violations bureau;
    (4) any statement made in the course of any proceedings under Rule 11 of the Rules of Criminal Procedure or equivalent procedure from another jurisdiction regarding the foregoing pleas;
    (5) any statement made in the course of plea discussions in which counsel for the prosecuting authority or for the defendant was a participant and that do not result in a plea of guilty or that result in a plea of guilty later withdrawn.

(B) A statement otherwise inadmissible under this rule is admissible in either of the following:

    (1) any proceeding in which another statement made in the course of the same plea or plea discussions has been introduced and the statement should, in fairness, be considered contemporaneously with it;
    (2) a criminal proceeding for perjury or false statement if the statement was made by the defendant under oath, on the record, and in the presence of counsel.

Rule 411. Liability Insurance

Evidence that a person was or was not insured against liability is not admissible upon the issue whether the person acted negligently or otherwise wrongfully. This rule does not require the exclusion of evidence of insurance against liability when offered for another purpose, such as proof of agency, ownership or control, if controverted, or bias or prejudice of a witness.

ART. V. PRIVILEGES

Rule 501. General Rule

The privilege of a witness, person, state or political subdivision thereof shall be governed by statute enacted by the General Assembly or by principles of common law as interpreted by the courts of this state in the light of reason and experience.

Rule 502. Attorney-Client Privilege and Work Product; Limitations on Waiver

The following provisions apply, in the circumstances set out, to disclosure of a communication or other information covered by the attorney-client privilege or work-product protection.

(A) Disclosure made in an Ohio proceeding or to an Ohio office or agency; Scope of waiver. When a disclosure is made in an Ohio proceeding or to an office or agency of an Ohio state, county, or local government that waives the attorney-client privilege or work-product protection, the waiver extends to an undisclosed communication or information in any proceeding only if:

(1) the waiver is intentional;

(2) the disclosed and undisclosed communications or information concern the same subject matter; and

(3) they ought in fairness to be considered together.

(B) Inadvertent Disclosure. When made in an Ohio proceeding or to an office or agency of an Ohio state, county, or local government, the disclosure does not operate as a waiver in any proceeding if:

(1) the disclosure is inadvertent;

(2) the holder of the privilege or protection took reasonable steps to prevent disclosure; and

(3) the holder promptly took reasonable steps to rectify the error, including (if applicable) following Ohio Civ.R. 26(B)(8)(b).

(C) Disclosure Made in Another Jurisdiction. When the disclosure is made in a proceeding in a federal court or the court of another state and is not the subject of a court order concerning waiver, the disclosure does not operate as a waiver in an Ohio proceeding if the disclosure:

(1) would not be a waiver under this rule if it had been made in an Ohio proceeding; or

(2) is not a waiver under the law governing the state or federal proceeding where the disclosure occurred.

(D) Controlling Effect of a Court Order. An Ohio court may order that the privilege or protection is not waived by disclosure connected with the litigation pending before the court, in which event the disclosure is also not a waiver in any other proceeding.

(E) Controlling effect of a party agreement. An agreement on the effect of a disclosure in an Ohio proceeding is binding only on the parties to the agreement, unless it is incorporated into a court order.

(F) Definitions. In this rule:

(1) "attorney-client privilege" means the protection that applicable law provides for confidential attorney-client communications; and

(2) "work-product protection" means the protection that applicable law provides for tangible material (or its intangible equivalent) prepared in anticipation of litigation or for trial.

ART. VI. WITNESSES

Rule 601. General Rule of Competency

(A) General rule. Every person is competent to be a witness except as otherwise provided in these rules.

(B) Disqualification of witness in general. A person is disqualified to testify as a
witness when the court determines that the person is:

    (1) Incapable of expressing himself or herself concerning the matter as to be
understood, either directly or through interpretation by one who can understand him or her; or

    (2) Incapable of understanding the duty of a witness to tell the truth.

    (3) A spouse testifying against the other spouse charged with a crime except when either of the following applies:

        (a) a crime against the testifying spouse or a child of either spouse is charged;

        (b) the testifying spouse elects to testify.

    (4) An officer, while on duty for the exclusive or main purpose of enforcing traffic laws, arresting or assisting in the arrest of a person charged with a traffic violation punishable as a misdemeanor where the officer at the time of the arrest was not using a properly marked motor vehicle as defined by statute or was not wearing a legally distinctive uniform as defined by statute.

    (5) A person giving expert testimony on the issue of liability in any medical claim, as defined in R.C. 2305.113, asserted in any civil action against a physician, podiatrist, or hospital arising out of the diagnosis, care, or treatment of any person by a physician or podiatrist, unless:

        (a) The person testifying is licensed to practice medicine and surgery, osteopathic medicine and surgery, or podiatric medicine and surgery by the state medical board or by the licensing authority of any state;

        (b) The person devotes at least one-half of his or her professional time to the active clinical practice in his or her field of licensure, or to its instruction in an accredited school and

        (c) The person practices in the same or a substantially similar specialty as the defendant. The court shall not permit an expert in one medical specialty to testify against a health care provider in another medical specialty unless the expert shows both that the standards of care and practice in the two specialties are similar and that the expert has substantial familiarity between the specialties.

If the person is certified in a specialty, the person must be certified by a board recognized by the American board of medical specialties or the American board of osteopathic specialties in a specialty having acknowledged expertise and training directly related to the particular health care matter at issue.

Nothing in this division shall be construed to limit the power of the trial court to adjudge the testimony of any expert witness incompetent on any other ground, or to limit the power of the trial court to allow the testimony of any other witness, on a matter unrelated to the liability issues in the medical claim, when that testimony is relevant to the medical claim involved.

This division shall not prohibit other medical professionals who otherwise are competent to testify under these rules from giving expert testimony on the appropriate standard of care in their own profession in any claim asserted in any civil action against a physician, podiatrist, medical professional, or hospital arising out of the diagnosis, care, or treatment of any person.
(6) As otherwise provided in these rules.

Rule 602. Lack of Personal Knowledge
A witness may not testify to a matter unless evidence is introduced sufficient to support a finding that the witness has personal knowledge of the matter. Evidence to prove personal knowledge may, but need not, consist of the witness' own testimony. This rule is subject to the provisions of Rule 703, relating to opinion testimony by expert witnesses.

Rule 603. Oath or Affirmation
Before testifying, every witness shall be required to declare that the witness will testify truthfully, by oath or affirmation administered in a form calculated to awaken the witness' conscience and impress the witness' mind with the duty to do so.

Rule 604. Interpreters
An interpreter is subject to the provisions of these rules relating to qualification as an expert and the administration of an oath or affirmation to make a true translation.

Rule 605. Competency of Judge as Witness
The judge presiding at the trial may not testify in that trial as a witness. No objection need be made in order to preserve the point.

Rule 606. Competency of Juror as Witness
(A) At the Trial. A member of the jury may not testify as a witness before that jury in the trial of the case in which the juror is sitting. If the juror is called so to testify, the opposing party shall be afforded an opportunity to object out of the presence of the jury.

(B) Inquiry into Validity of Verdict or Indictment.

    (1) Prohibited Testimony or other Evidence. Upon an inquiry into the validity of a verdict or indictment, <u>a juror may not testify</u> as to any <u>matter or statement occurring during</u> the course of the jury's <u>deliberations</u> or to the <u>effect</u> of anything upon that or any other juror's mind or emotions as influencing the juror to assent to or dissent from the verdict or indictment or concerning the juror's mental processes in connection therewith. A juror's <u>affidavit</u> or evidence of any statement by the juror concerning a matter about which the juror would be precluded from testifying <u>will not be received</u> by the court for these purposes.

    (2) Exceptions. <u>A juror may testify</u> about whether:

        (a) <u>extraneous prejudicial information</u> was improperly brought to the jury's attention;

        (b) any <u>outside influence</u> was improperly brought to bear on any juror; or,

        (c) <u>any threat, any bribe, any attempted threat or bribe</u>, or any improprieties of any officer of the court occurred.

Rule 607. Impeachment

(A) Who May Impeach. The credibility of a witness may be attacked by <u>any party</u> except that the credibility of a witness may be attacked by the party calling the witness by means of a prior inconsistent statement only upon a showing of surprise and affirmative damage. This exception does not apply to statements admitted pursuant to Evid.R. 801(D)(1)(a), 801(D)(2), or 803.

(B) Impeachment: Reasonable Basis. A questioner <u>must have a reasonable basis</u> for asking any question pertaining to impeachment that implies the existence of an impeaching fact.

Rule 608. Evidence of Character and Conduct of Witness

(A) Opinion and Reputation Evidence of Character. The credibility of a witness may be attacked or supported by evidence in the form of opinion or reputation, but subject to these limitations: (1) the evidence may refer <u>only to character for truthfulness or untruthfulness</u>, and (2) evidence of truthful character is admissible <u>only after</u> the character of the witness for truthfulness has been <u>attacked</u> by opinion or reputation evidence or otherwise.

(B) Specific Instances of Conduct. Specific instances of the conduct of a witness, for the purpose of attacking or supporting the witness's character for truthfulness, other than conviction of crime as provided in Evid.R. 609, <u>may not be proved by extrinsic evidence</u>. They may, however, in the <u>discretion</u> of the court, if clearly probative of truthfulness or untruthfulness, <u>be inquired into on cross</u>-examination of the witness (1) concerning the witness's character for truthfulness or untruthfulness, or (2) concerning the character for truthfulness or untruthfulness of another witness as to which character the witness being cross-examined has testified.

The giving of testimony by any witness, including an accused, does not operate as a waiver of the witness's privilege against self-incrimination when examined with respect to matters that relate only to the witness's character for truthfulness.

Rule 609. Impeachment by Evidence of Conviction of Crime

(A) General Rule. For the purpose of attacking the credibility of a witness:

(1) subject to Evid.R. 403, evidence that a witness <u>other than the accused</u> has been convicted of a crime is admissible if the <u>crime was punishable by death or imprisonment in excess of one year</u> pursuant to the law under which the witness was convicted.

(2) notwithstanding Evid.R. 403(A), but subject to Evid.R. 403(B), evidence that the <u>accused</u> has been convicted of a crime is admissible if the <u>crime was punishable by death or imprisonment in excess of one year</u> pursuant to the law under which the accused was convicted and if the court determines that the probative value of the evidence outweighs the danger of unfair prejudice, of confusion of the issues, or of misleading the jury.

(3) notwithstanding Evid.R. 403(A), but subject to Evid.R. 403(B), evidence that any witness, including an accused, has been convicted of a crime <u>is admissible</u> if the crime <u>involved dishonesty or false statement, regardless of the punishment</u> and whether based upon state or federal statute or local ordinance.

(B) Time Limit. Evidence of a conviction under this rule is not admissible <u>if a period of more than ten years has elapsed</u> since the date of the conviction or of the release of the witness from the <u>confinement,</u> or the termination of community control sanctions, post-release control, or <u>probation,</u> shock probation, <u>parole,</u> or shock parole imposed for that conviction, <u>whichever is the later date, unless</u> the court determines, in the interests of justice, that the probative value of the conviction supported by specific facts and circumstances substantially outweighs its prejudicial effect. However, evidence of a conviction more than ten years old as calculated herein, is not admissible unless the proponent gives to the adverse party sufficient advance written notice of intent to use such evidence to provide the adverse party with a fair opportunity to contest the use of such evidence.

(C) Effect of Pardon, Annulment, Expungement, or Certificate of Rehabilitation. Evidence of a <u>conviction is not admissible</u> under this rule if (1) the conviction has been the subject of a pardon, annulment, expungement, certificate of rehabilitation, or other equivalent procedure based on a finding of the rehabilitation of the person convicted, and that person has not been convicted of a subsequent crime which was punishable by death or imprisonment in excess of one year, or (2) the conviction has been the subject of a pardon, annulment, expungement, or other equivalent procedure based on a finding of innocence.

(D) Juvenile Adjudications. Evidence of juvenile adjudications is not admissible except as provided by statute enacted by the General Assembly.

(E) Pendency of Appeal. The pendency of an appeal therefrom does not render evidence of a conviction inadmissible. Evidence of the pendency of an appeal is admissible.

(F) Methods of Proof. When evidence of a witness's conviction of a crime is admissible under this rule, the fact of the conviction may be proved only by the testimony of the witness on direct or cross-examination, or by public record shown to the witness during his or her examination. If the witness denies that he or she is the person to whom the public record refers, the court may permit the introduction of additional evidence tending to establish that the witness is or is not the person to whom the public record refers.

Rule 610. Religious Beliefs or Opinions

Evidence of the beliefs or opinions of a witness on matters of religion is not admissible for the purpose of showing that by reason of their nature the witness' credibility is impaired or enhanced.

Rule 611. Mode and Order of Interrogation and Presentation

(A) Control by Court. The court shall exercise reasonable control over the mode and order of interrogating witnesses and presenting evidence so as to (1) make the interrogation and presentation effective for the ascertainment of the truth, (2) avoid needless consumption of time, and (3) protect witnesses from harassment or undue embarrassment.

(B) Scope of Cross-Examination. Cross-examination shall be permitted on all relevant matters and matters affecting credibility.

(C) Leading Questions. Leading questions should not be used on the direct examination of a witness except as may be necessary to develop the witness' testimony. Ordinarily leading questions should be permitted on cross-examination. When a party calls a hostile witness, an adverse party, or a witness identified with an adverse party, interrogation may be by leading questions.

Rule 612. Writing Used to Refresh Memory

If a witness uses a writing to refresh memory for the purpose of testifying, either: (1) while testifying;
or (2) before testifying, if the court in its discretion determines it is necessary in the interests of justice,
an adverse party is entitled to have the writing
produced at the hearing. The adverse party is also entitled
to inspect it,
to cross-examine the witness thereon, and
to introduce in evidence those portions which relate to the testimony of the witness.
If it is claimed that the writing contains matters not related to the subject matter of the testimony the court shall examine the writing in camera, excise any portions not so related, and order delivery of the remainder to the party entitled thereto. Any portion withheld over objections shall be preserved and made available to the appellate court in the event of an appeal. If a writing is not produced or delivered pursuant to order under this rule, the court shall make any order justice requires, except that in criminal cases when the prosecution elects not to comply, the order shall be one striking the testimony or, if the court in its discretion determines that the interests of justice so require, declaring a mistrial.

Rule 613. Impeachment by Self-Contradiction

(A) Examining Witness Concerning Prior Statement. In examining a witness concerning a prior statement made by the witness, whether <u>written or not</u>, the statement <u>need not be shown nor its contents disclosed to the witness</u> at that time, <u>but on request</u> the same shall be <u>shown or disclosed to opposing counsel</u>.

(B) Extrinsic Evidence of Prior Inconsistent Statement of Witness. Extrinsic evidence of a prior inconsistent statement by a witness is admissible if both of the following apply:

   (1) If the statement is offered solely for the purpose of impeaching the witness, the witness is afforded a prior opportunity to explain or deny the statement and the opposite party is afforded an opportunity to interrogate the witness on the statement or the interests of justice otherwise require;

   (2) The subject matter of the statement is one of the following:
      (a) A fact that is of consequence to the determination of the action other than the credibility of a witness;
      (b) A fact that may be shown by extrinsic evidence under Evid.R. 608(A), 609, 616(A), or 616(B);
      (c) A fact that may be shown by extrinsic evidence under the common law of impeachment if not in conflict with the Rules of Evidence.

(C) Prior Inconsistent Conduct. During examination of a witness, conduct of the witness inconsistent with the witness's testimony may be shown to impeach. If offered for the sole purpose of impeaching the witness's testimony, extrinsic evidence of the prior inconsistent conduct is admissible under the same circumstances as provided for prior inconsistent statements by Evid.R. 613(B)(2).

Rule 614. Calling and Interrogation of Witnesses by Court

(A) Calling by Court. The court may, on its own motion or at the suggestion of a party, call witnesses, and all parties are entitled to cross-examine witnesses thus called.

(B) Interrogation by Court. The court may interrogate witnesses, in an impartial manner, whether called by itself or by a party.

(C) Objections. Objections to the calling of witnesses by the court or to interrogation by it may be made at the time or at the next available opportunity when the jury is not present.

Rule 615. Separation and Exclusion of Witnesses

(A) Except as provided in division (B) of this rule, at the request of a party the court shall order witnesses excluded so that they cannot hear the testimony of other witnesses, and it may make the order of its own motion. An order directing the "exclusion" or "separation" of witnesses or the like, in general terms without specification of other or additional limitations, is effective only to require the exclusion of witnesses from the hearing during the testimony of other witnesses.

(B) This rule does not authorize exclusion of any of the following persons from the hearing:

(1) a party who is a natural person;

(2) an officer or employee of a party that is not a natural person designated as its representative by its attorney;

(3) a person whose presence is shown by a party to be essential to the presentation of the party's cause;

(4) in a criminal proceeding, a victim of the charged offense to the extent that the victim's presence is authorized by statute enacted by the General Assembly or by the Ohio Constitution. As used in this rule, "victim" has the same meaning as in the provisions of the Ohio Constitution providing rights for victims of crimes.

Rule 616 Methods of Impeachment

In addition to other methods, a witness may be impeached by any of the following methods:

(A) Bias. Bias, prejudice, interest, or any motive to misrepresent may be shown to impeach the witness either <u>by examination of the witness or by extrinsic evidence.</u>

(B) Sensory or Mental Defect. A defect of capacity, ability, or opportunity to observe, remember, or relate may be shown to impeach the witness either <u>by examination of the witness or by extrinsic evidence.</u>

(C) Specific Contradiction. Facts contradicting a witness's testimony may be shown for the purpose of impeaching the witness's testimony. <u>If</u> offered for the <u>sole purpose of impeaching</u> a witness's testimony, <u>extrinsic evidence of contradiction is inadmissible unless</u> the evidence is one of the following:

(1) Permitted by Evid. R. 608(A), 609, 613, 616(A), 616(B), or 706;

(2) Permitted by the common law of impeachment and not in conflict with the Rules of Evidence.

ART. VII. OPINIONS AND EXPERT TESTIMONY

Rule 701. Opinion Testimony by Lay Witnesses
If the witness is not testifying as an expert, the witness' testimony in the form of opinions or inferences is limited to those opinions or inferences which are (1) rationally based on the perception of the witness and (2) helpful to a clear understanding of the witness' testimony or the determination of a fact in issue.

Rule 702. Testimony by Experts
A witness may testify as an expert if the proponent demonstrates to the court that it is more likely than not that all of the following apply:
   (A) The witness' testimony either relates to matters beyond the knowledge or experience possessed by lay persons or dispels a misconception common among lay persons;
   (B) The witness is qualified as an expert by specialized knowledge, skill, experience, training, or education regarding the subject matter of the testimony;
   (C) The witness' testimony is based on reliable scientific, technical, or other specialized information and the expert's opinion reflects a reliable application of the principles and methods to the facts of the case. To the extent that the testimony reports the result of a procedure, test, or experiment, the testimony is reliable only if all of the following apply:
      (1) The theory upon which the procedure, test, or experiment is based is objectively verifiable or is validly derived from widely accepted knowledge, facts, or principles;
      (2) The design of the procedure, test, or experiment reliably implements the theory;
      (3) The particular procedure, test, or experiment was conducted in a way that will yield an accurate result.

Rule 703. Bases of Opinion Testimony by Experts
The facts or data in the particular case upon which an expert bases an opinion or inference may be those perceived by the expert or admitted in evidence at the hearing.

Rule 704. Opinion on Ultimate Issue
Testimony in the form of an opinion or inference otherwise admissible is not objectionable solely because it embraces an ultimate issue to be decided by the trier of fact.

Rule 705. Disclosure of Facts or Data Underlying Expert Opinion
The expert may testify in terms of opinion or inference and give the expert's reasons therefor after disclosure of the underlying facts or data. The disclosure may be in response to a hypothetical question or otherwise.

ART. VIII. Hearsay

Rule 801. Definitions
The following definitions apply under this article:
(A) Statement. A "statement" is (1) an oral or written assertion or (2) nonverbal conduct of a person, if it is intended by the person as an assertion.
(B) Declarant. A "declarant" is a person who makes a statement.
(C) Hearsay. "Hearsay" is a statement, other than one made by the declarant while testifying at the trial or hearing, <u>offered in evidence to prove the truth of the matter asserted in the statement</u>..
(D) Statements That Are Not Hearsay. A statement is not hearsay if:

    (1) Prior Statement by Witness. The <u>declarant testifies</u> at trial or hearing and is subject to <u>examination</u> concerning the statement, and the statement is

        (a) <u>inconsistent</u> with declarant's testimony, and was given <u>under oath</u> subject to <u>examination</u> by the <u>party against whom</u> the statement is offered and subject to the penalty of perjury at a trial, hearing, or other proceeding, or in a deposition, or

        (b) <u>consistent</u> with declarant's testimony and is <u>offered to rebut</u> an express or implied charge against declarant of recent fabrication or improper influence or motive, or

        (c) one of <u>identification</u> of a person soon after perceiving the person, if the circumstances demonstrate the reliability of the prior identification.

    (2) Admission by Party-Opponent. The statement is offered against a party and is

        (a) the party's <u>own statement</u>, in either an individual or a representative capacity, or

        (b) a statement of which the party has manifested an <u>adoption or belief</u> in its truth, or

        (c) a statement by a person <u>authorized</u> by the party to make a statement concerning the subject, or

        (d) a statement by the party's <u>agent</u> or servant concerning a matter <u>within the scope</u> of the agency or employment, made <u>during the existence</u> of the relationship, or

        (e) a statement by a <u>co-conspirator</u> of a party <u>during</u> the course and <u>in furtherance</u> of the conspiracy upon independent proof of the conspiracy.

Rule 802. Hearsay Rule
Hearsay is not admissible except as otherwise provided by the Constitution of the United States, by the Constitution of the State of Ohio, by statute enacted by the General Assembly not in conflict with a rule of the Supreme Court of Ohio, by these rules, or by other rules prescribed by the Supreme Court of Ohio.

Rule 803. Exceptions to The Rule Against Hearsay--Regardless of Whether the Declarant is Available as a Witness
The following are not excluded by the hearsay rule, even though the declarant is available as a witness:

(1) Present Sense Impression. A statement describing or explaining an event or condition made while the declarant was perceiving the event or condition, or immediately thereafter unless circumstances indicate lack of trustworthiness.

(2) Excited Utterance. A statement relating to a startling event or condition made while the declarant was under the stress of excitement caused by the event or condition.

(3) Then Existing, Mental, Emotional, or Physical Condition. A statement of the declarant's then existing state of mind, emotion, sensation, or physical condition (such as intent, plan, motive, design, mental feeling, pain, and bodily health), but not including a statement of memory or belief to prove the fact remembered or believed unless it relates to the execution, revocation, identification, or terms of declarant's will.

(4) Statements for Purposes of Medical Diagnosis or Treatment. Statements made for purposes of medical diagnosis or treatment and describing medical history, or past or present symptoms, pain, or sensations, or the inception or general character of the cause or external source thereof insofar as reasonably pertinent to diagnosis or treatment.

Rule 803(5). Recorded Recollection.

(5) Recorded Recollection. A memorandum or record concerning a matter about which a witness once had knowledge but now has insufficient recollection to enable him to testify fully and accurately, shown by the testimony of the witness to have been made or adopted when the matter was fresh in his memory and to reflect that knowledge correctly. If admitted, the memorandum or record may be read into evidence but may not itself be received as an exhibit unless offered by an adverse party.

(6) Records of Regularly Conducted Activity. A memorandum, report, record, or data compilation, in any form, of acts, events, or conditions, made at or near the time by, or from information transmitted by, a person with knowledge, if kept in the course of a regularly conducted business activity, and if it was the regular practice of that business activity to make the memorandum, report, record, or data compilation, all as shown by the testimony of the custodian or other qualified witness or as provided by Rule 901(B)(10), unless the source of information or the method or circumstances of preparation indicate lack of trustworthiness. The term "business" as used in this paragraph includes business, institution, association, profession, occupation, and calling of every kind, whether or not conducted for profit.

(7) Absence of Entry in Record Kept in Accordance with the Provisions of Paragraph (6). Evidence that a matter is not included in the memoranda, reports, records, or data compilations, in any form, kept in accordance with the provisions of paragraph (6), to prove the nonoccurrence or nonexistence of the matter, if the matter was of a kind of which a memorandum, report, record, or data compilation was regularly made and preserved, unless the sources of information or other circumstances indicate lack of trustworthiness.

(8) Public Records and Reports. Records, reports, statements, or data compilations, in any form, of public offices or agencies, setting forth (a) the activities of the office or agency, or (b) matters observed pursuant to duty imposed by law as to which matters there was a duty to report, excluding, however, in criminal cases matters observed by police officers and other law enforcement personnel, unless offered by defendant, unless the sources of information or other circumstances indicate lack of trustworthiness.

(9) Records of Vital Statistics. Records or data compilations, in any form, of births, fetal deaths, deaths, or marriages, if the report thereof was made to a public office pursuant to requirement of law
(10) Absence of Public Record. Testimony--or a certification under Evid.R. 901(B)(10)--that a diligent search failed to disclose a public record or statement if:
    (a) the testimony or certification is admitted to prove that
        (i) the record or statement does not exist; or
        (ii) a matter did not occur or exist, if a public office regularly kept a record or statement for a matter of that kind; and
    (b) in a criminal case, a prosecutor who intends to offer a certification provides written notice of that intent at least 14 days before trial, and the defendant does not object in writing within 7 days of receiving the notice--unless the court sets a different time for the notice or the objection.
(11) Records of Religious Organizations. Statements of births, marriages, divorces, deaths, legitimacy, ancestry, relationship by blood or marriage, or other similar facts of personal or family history, contained in a regularly kept record of a religious organization.
(12) Marriage, Baptismal, and Similar Certificates. Statements of fact contained in a certificate that the maker performed a marriage or other ceremony or administered a sacrament, made by a clergyman, public official, or other person authorized by the rules or practices of a religious organization or by law to perform the act certified, and purporting to have been issued at the time of the act or within a reasonable time thereafter.
(13) Family Records. Statements of fact concerning personal or family history contained in family Bibles, genealogies, charts, engravings on rings, inscriptions on family portraits, engravings on urns, crypts, or tombstones, or the like.
(14) Records of Documents Affecting an Interest in Property. The record of a document purporting to establish or affect an interest in property, as proof of the content of the original recorded document and its execution and delivery by each person by whom it purports to have been executed, if the record is a record of a public office and an applicable statute authorizes the recording of documents of that kind in that office.

(15) Statements in Documents Affecting an Interest in Property. A statement contained in a document purporting to establish or affect an interest in property if the matter stated was relevant to the purpose of the document, unless dealings with the property since the document was made have been inconsistent with the truth of the statement or the purport of the document.

(16) Statements in Ancient Documents. Statements in a document that was prepared before January 1, 1998, and whose authenticity is established.

(17) Market Reports, Commercial Publications. Market quotations, tabulations, lists, directories, or other published compilations, generally used and relied upon by the public or by persons in particular occupations.

(18) Learned Treatises. To the extent <u>called to the attention</u> of an expert witness <u>upon cross</u>-examination or <u>relied upon</u> by the expert witness <u>in direct</u> examination, statements contained in published treatises, periodicals, or pamphlets on a subject of history, medicine, or other science or art, established as a reliable authority by the testimony or admission of the witness or by other expert testimony or by judicial notice. If admitted, the statements may be <u>read</u> into evidence but may <u>not be received</u> as exhibits.

(19) Reputation Concerning Personal or Family History. Reputation among members of the declarant's family by blood, adoption, or marriage or among the declarant's associates, or in the community, concerning a person's birth, adoption, marriage, divorce, death, legitimacy, relationship by blood, adoption or marriage, ancestry, or other similar fact of the declarant's personal or family history.

(20) Reputation Concerning Boundaries or General History. Reputation in a community, arising before the controversy, as to boundaries of or customs affecting lands in the community, and reputation as to events of general history important to the community or state or nation in which located.

(21) Reputation as to Character. Reputation of a person's character among the person's associates or in the community.

Rule 804. Hearsay Exceptions; Declarant Unavailable

(22) Judgment of Previous Conviction. Evidence of a final judgment, entered after a trial or upon a plea of guilty (but not upon a plea of no contest or the equivalent plea from another jurisdiction), adjudging a person guilty of a crime punishable by death or imprisonment in excess of one year, to prove any fact essential to sustain the judgment, but not including, when offered by the Government in a criminal prosecution for purposes other than impeachment, judgments against persons other than the accused. The pendency of an appeal may be shown but does not affect admissibility.

(23) Judgment as to Personal Family or General History, or Boundaries. Judgments as proof of matters of personal, family or general history, or boundaries, essential to the judgment, if the same would be provable by evidence of reputation.

Rule 804. Hearsay Exceptions; Declarant Unavailable
(A) Definition of Unavailability. "Unavailability as a witness" includes any of the following situations in which the declarant:
    (1) is exempted by ruling of the court on the ground of privilege from testifying concerning the subject matter of the declarant's statement;
    (2) persists in refusing to testify concerning the subject matter of the declarant's statement despite an order of the court to do so;
    (3) testifies to a lack of memory of the subject matter of the declarant's statement;
    (4) is unable to be present or to testify at the hearing because of death or then-existing physical or mental illness or infirmity;
    (5) is absent from the hearing and the proponent of the declarant's statement has been unable to procure the declarant's attendance (or in the case of a hearsay exception under division (B)(2), (3), or (4) of this rule, the declarant's attendance or testimony) by process or other reasonable means.
A declarant is not unavailable as a witness if the declarant's exemption, refusal, claim of lack of memory, inability, or absence is due to the procurement or wrongdoing of the proponent of the declarant's statement for the purpose of preventing the witness from attending or testifying.

(B) Hearsay Exceptions. The following are not excluded by the hearsay rule if the declarant is unavailable as a witness:

(1) Former Testimony. Testimony given as a witness at another hearing of the same or a different proceeding, or in a deposition taken in compliance with law in the course of the same or another proceeding, if the party against whom the testimony is now offered, or, in a civil action or proceeding, a predecessor in interest, had an opportunity and similar motive to develop the testimony by direct, cross, or redirect examination. Testimony given at a preliminary hearing must satisfy the right to confrontation and exhibit indicia of reliability.

(2) Statement Under Belief of Impending Death. In a prosecution for homicide or in a civil action or proceeding, a statement made by a declarant, while believing that his or her death was imminent, concerning the cause or circumstances of what the declarant believed to be his or her impending death.

(3) Statement Against Interest. A statement that was at the time of its making so far contrary to the declarant's pecuniary or proprietary interest, or so far tended to subject the declarant to civil or criminal liability, or to render invalid a claim by the declarant against another, that a reasonable person in the declarant's position would not have made the statement unless the declarant believed it to be true. A statement tending to expose the declarant to criminal liability, whether offered to exculpate or inculpate the accused, is not admissible unless corroborating circumstances clearly indicate the trustworthiness of the statement.

(4) Statement of Personal or Family History. (a) A statement concerning the declarant's own birth, adoption, marriage, divorce, legitimacy, relationship by blood, adoption, or marriage, ancestry, or other similar fact of personal or family history, even though the declarant had no means of acquiring personal knowledge of the matter stated; or (b) a statement concerning the foregoing matters, and death also, of another person, if the declarant was related to the other by blood, adoption, or marriage or was so intimately associated with the other's family as to be likely to have accurate information concerning the matter declared.

(5) Statement by a Deceased or Incompetent Person. The statement was made by a decedent or a mentally incompetent person, where all of the following apply:
    (a) the estate or personal representative of the decedent's estate or the guardian or trustee of the incompetent person is a party;
    (b) the statement was made before the death or the development of the incompetency;
    (c) the statement is offered to rebut testimony by an adverse party on a matter within the knowledge of the decedent or incompetent person.

(6) Forfeiture by Wrongdoing. A statement offered against a party if the unavailability of the witness is due to the wrongdoing of the party for the purpose of preventing the witness from attending or testifying. However, a statement is not admissible under this rule unless the proponent has given to each adverse party advance written notice of an intention to introduce the statement sufficient to provide the adverse party a fair opportunity to contest the admissibility of the statement.

Rule 805. Hearsay Within Hearsay
Hearsay included within hearsay is not excluded under the hearsay rule if each part of the combined statements conforms with an exception to the hearsay rule provided in these rules.

Rule 806. Attacking and Supporting Credibility of Declarant
(A) When a hearsay statement, or a statement defined in Evid.R. 801(D)(2), (c), (d), or (e), has been admitted in evidence, the credibility of the declarant may be attacked, and if attacked may be supported, by any evidence that would be admissible for those purposes if declarant had testified as a witness.
(B) Evidence of a statement or conduct by the declarant at any time, inconsistent with the declarant's hearsay statement, is not subject to any requirement that the declarant may have been afforded an opportunity to deny or explain.
(C) Evidence of a declarant's prior conviction is not subject to any requirement that the declarant be shown a public record.
(D) If the party against whom a hearsay statement has been admitted calls the declarant as a witness, the party is entitled to examine the declarant on the statement as if under cross-examination.

Rule 807. Hearsay Exceptions; Child Statements in Abuse Cases

(A) An out-of-court statement made by a child who is under twelve years of age at the time of trial or hearing describing any sexual activity performed, or attempted to be performed, by, with, or on the child or describing any act or attempted act of physical harm directed against the child's person is not excluded as hearsay under Evid.R. 802 if all of the following apply:

(1) The court finds that the totality of the circumstances surrounding the making of the statement provides particularized guarantees of trustworthiness that make the statement at least as reliable as statements admitted pursuant to Evid.R. 803 and 804. The circumstances must establish that the child was particularly likely to be telling the truth when the statement was made and that the test of cross-examination would add little to the reliability of the statement. In making its determination of the reliability of the statement, the court shall consider all of the circumstances surrounding the making of the statement, including but not limited to spontaneity, the internal consistency of the statement, the mental state of the child, the child's motive or lack of motive to fabricate, the child's use of terminology unexpected of a child of similar age, the means by which the statement was elicited, and the lapse of time between the act and the statement. In making this determination, the court shall not consider whether there is independent proof of the sexual activity or attempted sexual activity, or of the act or attempted act of physical harm directed against the child's person;

(2) The child's testimony is not reasonably obtainable by the proponent of the statement;

(3) There is independent proof of the sexual activity or attempted sexual activity, or of the act or attempted act of physical harm directed against the child's person;

(4) At least ten days before the trial or hearing, a proponent of the statement has notified all other parties in writing of the content of the statement, the time and place at which the statement was made, the identity of the witness who is to testify about the statement, and the circumstances surrounding the statement that are claimed to indicate its trustworthiness.

(B) The child's testimony is "not reasonably obtainable by the proponent of the statement" under division (A)(2) of this rule only if one or more of the following apply:

(1) The child refuses to testify concerning the subject matter of the statement or claims a lack of memory of the subject matter of the statement after a person trusted by the child, in the presence of the court, urges the child to both describe the acts described by the statement and to testify.
(2) The court finds all of the following:
    (a) the child is absent from the trial or hearing;
    (b) the proponent of the statement has been unable to procure the child's attendance or testimony by process or other reasonable means despite a good faith effort to do so;
    (c) it is probable that the proponent would be unable to procure the child's testimony or attendance if the trial or hearing were delayed for a reasonable time.
(3) The court finds both of the following:
(a) the child is unable to testify at the trial or hearing because of death or then existing physical or mental illness or infirmity;
(b) the illness or infirmity would not improve sufficiently to permit the child to testify if the trial or hearing were delayed for a reasonable time.

The proponent of the statement has not established that the child's testimony or attendance is not reasonably obtainable if the child's refusal, claim of lack of memory, inability, or absence is due to the procurement or wrongdoing of the proponent of the statement for the purpose of preventing the child from attending or testifying.
(C) The court shall make the findings required by this rule on the basis of a hearing conducted outside the presence of the jury and shall make findings of fact, on the record, as to the bases for its ruling.

ART. IX. AUTHENTICATION AND IDENTIFICATION

Rule 901. Requirement of Authentication or Identification
(A) General Provision. The requirement of authentication or identification as a condition precedent to admissibility is satisfied by evidence sufficient to support a finding that the matter in question is what its proponent claims.
(B) Illustrations. By way of illustration only, and not by way of limitation, the following are examples of authentication or identification conforming with the requirements of this rule:

Rule 901. Requirement of Authentication or Identification

(1) Testimony of Witness with Knowledge. Testimony that a matter is what it is claimed to be.

(2) Nonexpert Opinion on Handwriting. Nonexpert opinion as to the genuineness of handwriting, based upon familiarity not acquired for purposes of the litigation.

(3) Comparison by Trier or Expert Witness. Comparison by the trier of fact or by expert witness with specimens which have been authenticated.

(4) Distinctive Characteristics and the Like. Appearance, contents, substance, internal patterns, or other distinctive characteristics, taken in conjunction with circumstances.

(5) Voice Identification. Identification of a voice, whether heard firsthand or through mechanical or electronic transmission or recording, by opinion based upon hearing the voice at any time under circumstances connecting it with the alleged speaker.

(6) Telephone Conversations. Telephone conversations, by evidence that a call was made to the number assigned at the time by the telephone company to a particular person or business, if (a) in the case of a person, circumstances, including self-identification, show the person answering to be the one called, or (b) in the case of a business, the call was made to a place of business and the conversation related to business reasonably transacted over the telephone.

(7) Public Records or Reports. Evidence that a writing authorized by law to be recorded or filed and in fact recorded or filed in a public office, or a purported public record, report, statement or data compilation, in any form, is from the public office where items of this nature are kept.

(8) Ancient Documents or Data Compilation. Evidence that a document or data compilation, in any form, (a) is in such condition as to create no suspicion concerning its authenticity, (b) was in a place where it, if authentic, would likely be, and (c) has been in existence twenty years or more at the time it is offered.

(9) Process or System. Evidence describing a process or system used to produce a result and showing that the process or system produces an accurate result.

(10) Methods Provided by Statute or Rule. Any method of authentication or identification provided by statute enacted by the General Assembly not in conflict with a rule of the Supreme Court of Ohio or by other rules prescribed by the Supreme Court.

Rule 902. Self-Authentication

Extrinsic evidence of authenticity as a condition precedent to admissibility is not required with respect to the following:

(1) Domestic Public Documents Under Seal. A document bearing a seal purporting to be that of the United States, or of any State, district, Commonwealth, territory, or insular possession thereof, or the Panama Canal Zone, or the Trust Territory of the Pacific Islands, or of a political subdivision, department, officer, or agency thereof, and a signature purporting to be an attestation or execution.

(2) Domestic Public Documents Not Under Seal. A document purporting to bear the signature in the official capacity of an officer or employee of any entity included in paragraph (1) hereof, having no seal, if a public officer having a seal and having official duties in the district or political subdivision of the officer or employee certifies under seal that the signer has the official capacity and that the signature is genuine.

(3) Foreign Public Documents. A document purporting to be executed or attested in the official capacity by a person authorized by the laws of a foreign country to make the execution or attestation, and accompanied by a final certification as to the genuineness of the signature and official position (a) of the executing or attesting person, or (b) of any foreign official whose certificate of genuineness of signature and official position relates to the execution or attestation or is in a chain of certificates of genuineness of signature and official position relating to the execution or attestation. A final certification may be made by a secretary of embassy or legation, consul general, consul, vice consul, or consular agent of the United States, or a diplomatic or consular official of the foreign country assigned or accredited to the United States. If reasonable opportunity has been given to all parties to investigate the authenticity and accuracy of official documents, the court may, for good cause shown, order that they be treated as presumptively authentic without final certification or permit them to be evidenced by an attested summary with or without final certification.

Rule 902(4). Certified Copies of Public Records.

(4) Certified Copies of Public Records. A copy of an official record or report or entry therein, or of a document authorized by law to be recorded or filed and actually recorded or filed in a public office, including data compilations in any form, certified as correct by the custodian or other person authorized to make the certification, by certificate complying with paragraph (1), (2), or (3) of this rule or complying with any law of a jurisdiction, state or federal, or rule prescribed by the Supreme Court of Ohio.

(5) Official Publications. Books, pamphlets, or other publications purporting to be issued by public authority.

(6) Newspapers and Periodicals. Printed materials purporting to be newspapers or periodicals, including notices and advertisements contained therein.

(7) Trade Inscriptions and the Like. Inscriptions, signs, tags, or labels purporting to have been affixed in the course of business and indicating ownership, control, or origin.

(8) Acknowledged Documents. Documents accompanied by a certificate of acknowledgment executed in the manner provided by law by a notary public or other officer authorized by law to take acknowledgments.

(9) Commercial Paper and Related Documents. Commercial paper, signatures thereon, and documents relating thereto to the extent provided by general commercial law.

(10) Presumptions Created by Law. Any signature, document, or other matter declared by any law of a jurisdiction, state or federal, to be presumptively or prima facie genuine or authentic.

(11) Certified Domestic Records of a Regularly Conducted Activity. The original or a copy of a domestic record that meets the requirements of Evid.R. 803(6), as shown <u>by a certification</u> of the custodian or another qualified person that complies with an Ohio statute or a rule prescribed by the Supreme Court of Ohio. Before the trial or hearing, the proponent <u>must give</u> an adverse party <u>reasonable written notice</u> of the intent to offer the record - <u>and must make the record and certification available for inspection</u> - so that the party has a fair opportunity to challenge them.

Rule 902(12). Certified Foreign Records of a Regularly Conducted Activity.

(12) Certified Foreign Records of a Regularly Conducted Activity. In a civil case, the original or a copy of a foreign record that meets the requirements of Evid.R. 902(11), modified as follows: the certification, rather than complying with an Ohio statute or Supreme Court of Ohio rule, must be signed in a manner that, if falsely made, would subject the maker to a criminal penalty in the country where the certification is signed. The proponent must also meet the notice requirements of Evid.R. 902(11).

(13) Certified Records Generated by an Electronic Process or System. A record generated by an electronic process or system that produces an accurate result, as shown by a certification of a qualified person that complies with the certification requirements of Evid.R. 902(11) or (12). The proponent must also meet the notice requirements of Evid.R. 902(11).

(14) Certified Data Copied from an Electronic Device, Storage Medium, or File. Data copied from an electronic device, storage medium, or file, if authenticated by a process of digital identification, as shown by a certification of a qualified person that complies with the certification requirements of Evid.R. 902(11) or (12). The proponent also must meet the notice requirements of Evid.R. 902(11).

Rule 903. Subscribing Witness' Testimony Unnecessary
The testimony of a subscribing witness is not necessary to authenticate a writing unless required by the laws of the jurisdiction whose laws govern the validity of the writing.

ART. X. CONTENTS OF WRITINGS, RECORDINGS AND PHOTOGRAPHS

Rule 1001. Definitions
For purposes of this article the following definitions are applicable:

(1) **Writings and Recordings.** "Writings" and "recordings" consist of letters, words, or numbers, or their equivalent, set down by handwriting, typewriting, printing, photostating, photographing, magnetic impulse, mechanical or electronic recording, or other forms of data compilation.

(2) **Photographs.** "Photographs" include still photographs, X-ray films, video tapes, and motion pictures.

(3) **Original.** An "original" of a writing or recording is the writing or recording itself or any counterpart <u>intended to have the same effect</u> by a person executing or issuing it. An "original" of a photograph includes the <u>negative or any print</u> therefrom. If data are stored in a computer or similar device, any printout or other output readable by sight, shown to reflect the data accurately, is an "original."

(4) **Duplicate.** A "duplicate" is a counterpart produced by the same impression as the original, or from the same matrix, or by means of photography, including enlargements and miniatures, or by mechanical or electronic re-recording, or by chemical reproduction, or by other equivalent techniques which accurately reproduce the original. A "duplicate" includes a counterpart from which personal identifiers have been omitted pursuant to Rule 45 of the Rules of Superintendence for the Courts of Ohio, and which otherwise accurately reproduces the original.

Rule 1002. Requirement of Original
<u>To prove the content</u> of a writing, recording, or photograph, <u>the original</u> writing, recording, or photograph <u>is required</u>, except as otherwise provided in these rules or by statute enacted by the General Assembly not in conflict with a rule of the Supreme Court of Ohio.

Rule 1003. Admissibility of Duplicates
A duplicate is admissible to the same extent as an original unless (1) a genuine question is raised as to the authenticity of the original or (2) in the circumstances it would be unfair to admit the duplicate in lieu of the original.

Rule 1004. Admissibility of Other Evidence of Contents

The original is not required, and other evidence of the contents of a writing, recording, or photograph is admissible if:

(1) Originals Lost or Destroyed. All originals are lost or have been destroyed, unless the proponent lost or destroyed them in bad faith; or

(2) Original Not Obtainable. No original can be obtained by any available judicial process or procedure; or

(3) Original in Possession of Opponent. At a time when an original was under the control of the party against whom offered, that party was put on notice, by the pleadings or otherwise, that the contents would be subject of proof at the hearing, and that party does not produce the original at the hearing; or

(4) Collateral Matters. The writing, recording, or photograph is not closely related to a controlling issue.

Rule 1005. Public Records

The contents of an official record, or of a document authorized to be recorded or filed and actually recorded or filed, including data compilations in any form if otherwise admissible, may be proved by copy, certified as correct in accordance with Rule 902, Civ. R. 44, Crim. R. 27 or testified to be correct by a witness who has compared it with the original. If a copy which complies with the foregoing cannot be obtained by the exercise of reasonable diligence, then other evidence of the contents may be given.

Rule 1006 Summaries

The contents of voluminous writings, recordings, or photographs which cannot conveniently be examined in court may be presented in the form of a chart, summary, or calculation. The originals, or duplicates, shall be made available for examination or copying, or both, by other parties at a reasonable time and place. The court may order that they be produced in court.

Rule 1007 Testimony or Written Admission of Party

Contents of writings, recordings, or photographs may be proved by the testimony or deposition of the party against whom offered or by that party's written admission, without accounting for the nonproduction of the original.

Rule 1008. Functions of Court and Jury

When the admissibility of other evidence of contents of writings, recordings, or photographs under these rules depends upon the fulfillment of a condition of fact, the question whether the condition has been fulfilled is ordinarily for the court to determine in accordance with the provisions of Rule 104. However, when an issue is raised (a) whether the asserted writing ever existed, or (b) whether another writing, recording, or photograph produced at the trial is the original, or (c) whether other evidence of contents correctly reflects the contents, the issue is for the trier of fact to determine as in the case of other issues of fact.

ART. XI. MISCELLANEOUS RULES

Rule 1101. [Reserved]

Rule 1102. Effective date

(A) Effective Date of Rules. These rules shall take effect on the first day of July 1980. ..

(B)- (V) Effective Date of Amendments. ...[removed by author] 1981 to July 1, 2020.

Rule 1103. Title

These rules shall be known as the Ohio Rules of Evidence and may be cited as "Evidence Rules" or "Evid.R. ___."

Making and Responding to Common Objections

Professor John Barkai

> This section of the handbook provides ideas about making and responding to common objections, and it also includes a list of common objections.

There is almost an endless number of objections that could be made at a trial. There are many lists or "cheat sheets" of objections that can be found on the Internet and many articles about objections. This section of the handbook will discuss the basics about objections and provide a list of the more common objections.

Why Do Lawyers Object?
Lawyers object during trial to:

1) control the information that the fact finder can consider
   (to exclude testimony or exhibits offered by the opposing party),

2) control the opposing lawyer's conduct
   (to prevent certain questions or answers, prevent the calling of certain witnesses, prevent certain statements from being made during opening statements or closing arguments),

3) preserve errors for appeal,

4) disrupt opponent's counsel's momentum,

5) send a signal to a witness,

6) communicate with the fact finder, and

7) give the witness a break and time to think.

Lawyers frequently object to the form of question (Argumentative, Ambiguous, Vague, Asked and Answered, etc.) to prevent the judge or jury from hearing inadmissible evidence. Often, however, such objections are made simply to harass, annoy, upset, or distract opposing counsel. The less experience the lawyer doing trials has, the more such objections are likely to distract them. Some people consider objections made for such purposes to be "unethical;" other people consider such objections part of the competition in the adversary system. Whatever your view, be ready for such objections.

Make an Objection in Four Steps
1) Stand up.
2) Say, "Objection _____" (Fill in the blank with your reason).
3) Identify your specific objection.
   a) At a minimum, say the topic type
      (Hearsay, Relevance, Improper Impeachment, Improper Character, Lack of Foundation, Leading Question, etc.)
   b) State the evidence rule number if you know it (R404, etc.).
   c) A combination of the above
      ("Objection, Improper Impeachment, R613")
4) Stop talking and listen to the judge.
   Be prepared to state reasons for your objection and to make an argument to support your position.

How to Respond to an Objection
1) Speak to the judge, not the lawyer who objected.
2) Explain to the judge why your evidence should be admissible. ("Your Honor, that statement is not hearsay because I am not offering it for the truth, but rather to show notice.")
3) If you recognize that you did not lay an appropriate foundation for the evidence, explain that you will do that. ("Your Honor, I will lay the foundation.")
4) If you recognize that the opposing counsel was objecting to the form of your question, which most often happens on your direct examination, simply say, "I'll rephrase." Rephrase the question and move on with your witness examination. Do not get sidetracked by the opposing counsel who might have objected just to throw you off track.
5) For any physical piece of evidence, statement, or testimony that you will be introducing, prepare in advance and have a reason why you believe that evidence is admissible. Be ready to make that argument to the judge.
6) If the objection is to relevance, and you think you will be able to show that it is relevant after additional testimony, say to the judge, "I will connect it up in a few questions Your Honor." Such a statement is equivalent of saying "trust me." If you do say that, you had better connect it up later or the judge will not trust you in the future.

If You are a Judge Who Has to Rule on the Objection
1) If the specific objection was not identified, turn to the lawyer who made the objection and say, "Basis?" - Meaning, "What is the legal basis for your objection?"
2) After the lawyer has put their specific objection on the record, turn to the proponent (the lawyer who is attempting to introduce the evidence), and say, "What is your response?"
3) Allow more argument if necessary. "Counsel, how do you respond to that argument?"
4) After the arguments are completed, make your ruling.
   A) "Sustained" - meaning you agree with the objection, and you will exclude the evidence.
   B) "Overruled" - meaning you agree with the proponent of the evidence, and the evidence will be admissible.
   C) Reserve your ruling until the end of the trial. ("I will reserve my decision on this issue until the close of the testimony.")
   D) Ask lawyers to submit a written memorandum on the issue when the trial ends so you have a better understanding of the issue.

Multiple Lawyers and Multiple Clients
If two or more lawyers represent one client, only one of the lawyers can object to each of the witnesses. Only one lawyer can make objections for each witness, e.g. if you do the direct, you are the only one who can object on cross. They cannot "tag team" and both object or respond to objections for single witness. If there are multiple parties who each have their own lawyer, each lawyer must make their own objection to have the objections preserved for appeal.

Judges Apply the Rules of Evidence More Loosely in Nonjury Trials. Many jurisdictions apply a presumption that a trial judge will ignore inadmissible evidence. I doubt that is true. What is to the questionable evidence is very seldom basis for reversing a verdict in a nonjury trial.

The Key to Objections is Rule 103 There is a rhyme to this phrase. "Key" rhymes with "103." Rule 103 holds the key to understanding the process of objections. Read that rule very carefully. The full rule follows.

Important Points about Rule 103 include:
1) The objection must be timely and state the specific ground for the objection, unless it is apparent from the context.
2) If the evidence was admitted, appellate courts do not have to consider the issue unless a specific ground for the objection was timely stated.
3) If the evidence was excluded, the appellate court needs information about what the excluded evidence was going to be. That information must be provided by an "offer of proof" unless the information was apparent from the context.
4) The judge can make statements for the record about the objection, the evidence, the form of the evidence, the ruling, and can require an offer of proof in question and answer form.
5) An error is not sufficient to reverse the trial unless a "substantial right" of a party is affected.
6) Even if there was no objection at trial, "plain errors" affecting "substantial rights" can result in a reversal on appeal.

Ohio Rule 103. Rulings on Evidence
(A) Effect of Erroneous Ruling. Error may not be predicated upon a ruling which admits or excludes evidence unless a substantial right of the party is affected; and
>**(1) Objection.** In case the ruling is one admitting evidence, a timely objection or motion to strike appears of record, stating the specific ground of objection, if the specific ground was not apparent from the context; or
>**(2) Offer of Proof.** In case the ruling is one excluding evidence, the substance of the evidence was made known to the court by offer or was apparent from the context within which questions were asked. Offer of proof is not necessary if evidence is excluded during cross-examination.

Once the court rules definitely on the record, either before or at trial, a party need not renew an objection or offer of proof to preserve a claim of error for appeal.
(B) Record of Offer and Ruling. At the time of making the ruling, the court may add any other or further statement which shows the character of the evidence, the form in which it was offered, the objection made, and the ruling thereon. It may direct the making of an offer in question and answer form.
(C) Hearing of Jury. In jury cases, proceedings shall be conducted, to the extent practicable, so as to prevent inadmissible evidence from being suggested to the jury by any means, such as making statements or offers of proof or asking questions in the hearing of the jury.
(D) Plain Error. Nothing in this rule precludes taking notice of plain errors affecting substantial rights although they were not brought to the attention of the court.

The Most Common Substantive Objections Are Based on The Rules of Evidence and Constitutional Issues. Each article within the evidence code has one or more common types of objections, such as:

General provisions	100s
Objections	
Preliminary questions	
Limited admissibility	
Remainder of or related writings	
Judicial notice	200s
Presumptions	300s
Relevance	400s
Privileges	500s
Witnesses	600s
Competence	
Impeachment	
Opinions and expert testimony	700s
Hearsay	800s
Authentication	900s
Best evidence (original writings)	1000s

Motions in Limine

In a jury trial, lawyers often make a pretrial motion in limine, which is a motion to exclude or admit certain evidence. In jury trials, the motion is made outside the presence of the jury. The judge's ruling on the motion in limine can 1) prevent inadmissible evidence from being heard by a jury, or 2) allow lawyers to know that they can go forward and attempt to introduce certain evidence without risking a mistrial. Motions in limine are probably not necessary in a nonjury trial because the judge will have to hear the potentially inadmissible evidence before ruling on the motion. Therefore, even if the evidence would be ruled inadmissible, the trial judge who will be the trier of fact will have already heard the inadmissible evidence. Judges in nonjury trials are presumed to ignore inadmissible evidence.

Phrases and Questions that Suggest Inadmissible or Objectionable Information is Coming.

Lawyer: "In summary, witness you've testified that…"
Likely objection: Asked and answered

Lawyer: "Witness, what if I told you that another witness testified that…"
Likely objection: Calls for speculation, argumentative, etc.

Inadequate Objections – Not Specific Enough
"I object."
"Objection to the form of the question."
"Insufficient foundation."
"Inadmissible."
"Incompetent, irrelevant, and immaterial."

Offers of Proof are:
1) sometimes just summary statements by a lawyer of what the evidence would be if the lawyer were given an opportunity to call the witness or introduce the exhibit. ("Your Honor, if the witness would be allowed to testify, she would say that ……"), and,
2) sometimes offers of proof are questions of the lawyer and answers of the witness given in question and answer form outside the presence of the jury. (Q1 A1; Q2 A2; Q3 A3)

The Impact of Objections in Nonjury Trials – Seldom Reversed
Many objections, especially to the forms of questions, seldom result in reversals even in jury trials. It would be extremely rare for an appellate court to reverse a nonjury trial decision based on an objection to the form of a question or the form of an answer. Although objection battles on the forms of questions do take place in jury trials, such battles are less important in nonjury trials because the judge is presumed to ignore inadmissible evidence and decide the case only on evidence that was admissible.

Common Phrases from Court Opinions Summarizing That Inadmissible Evidence in A Nonjury Trial Will Not Result in A Reversal Include:
- "Trial judges often have access to inadmissible and highly prejudicial information and are presumed to be able to discount or disregard it."
- "In bench trials, judges routinely hear inadmissible evidence that they are presumed to ignore."
- "The presumption that the trial judge disregarded all inadmissible evidence in reaching his decision."
- "It is presumed that improper evidence taken under objection was given no weight in reaching the final conclusion [in a nonjury trial] unless the contrary appears."
- "A judge, as factfinder, is presumed to disregard inadmissible evidence and consider only competent evidence."
- "A judge "must be presumed to be able to disregard inflammatory evidence"

Common Objections to the Form of the Question

Objections to the form of the question often have no clear answers or standards. Many judges and lawyers might disagree as to whether some question is improper or not. If a rule is cited when making the objection, it would usually be Rule 611.

Argumentative (also called **Harassing, Badgering**) **(R611)**
An argumentative question asks the witness to accept the examiner's summary, inference, or conclusion rather than a fact. Often the objector is trying to protect a witness during cross-examination.
Examples of Argumentative Questions:
"Isn't what you told this judge on its face ridiculous?"
"How can you expect the judge to believe that?"
"Are you telling this court that you don't know what a machete is?"
"Do you really expect the judge to believe that?"
"Do you mean to tell me...?"
"Doesn't it seem strange that...?"
"Your kind of the hatchet man down here for the D.A.s Office, aren't you?"
"It wouldn't bother you any, to come in here and lie from the time you started to the time you stopped, would it?"

Asked and Answered: This rule is violated by repeating the same question, asked by the same lawyer, to get the same answer, from the same witness, and is not permitted under R611. A question which has previously been asked and answered is being asked again. The rule prevents cumulative testimony R403. Repeating the testimony of a witness who has previously given the same testimony after being asked the same question by the same lawyer in not permitted. However, similar questions are often permitted if the identical information is not repeated. This objection does not apply to prevent the same questions being asked on cross-examination that were asked on direct examination. It does not prevent asking identical questions of different witnesses, nor does it prevent a lawyer representing a co-party from asking the same questions to the same witness again.

Assuming Facts Not in Evidence. This rule is violated when part of a question (usually the first part) assumes the truth of a fact that is in dispute but has not yet been proved at trial. Such a question is unfair because it cannot be answered without conceding the unproven fact. Assuming facts not in evidence may be an attempt to bring into the trial information that the lawyer is not able to prove by other means. However, questions that assume facts are permitted on cross-examination to impeach a witness's credibility.

Examples of assuming facts not in evidence:
"When did you stop beating your wife?" (assumes previous beatings)
"Did you know their business dropped 50% because of what the defendant did?" (assumes the defendant did the same thing)
"How long after you purchased the items were they given to the defendant?" (assumes the purchase)

Responses:
"I will connect it up later."(Which just means, "Judge trust me and allow a few more questions." And, if you request permission to "connect up later" you'd better be able to connect it up or the judge will no longer trust you.)
"I have a good faith basis for assuming those facts. I would like to proceed without further tipping my hand."
"This is criminal case and the defendant has a Sixth Amendment right to fully cross-examine the witness."

Beyond the Scope (of a prior examination). Questions on redirect examination cannot go into subject matters that have not been covered in the previous cross-examination. Similarly, questions on re-cross examination cannot go beyond the scope of redirect examination. Redirect examination is limited to issues raised by the opposing lawyer on cross-examination. If the questions go beyond the issues raised on cross, the objection will be valid.

Responses.
"Your Honor, I'm allowed to go into this area because it goes to the witness's credibility."

Note well: Cross-examination is not limited to the subjects covered on direct examination. If it were so limited, the cross examiner would be prohibited from fully examining the witness and exposing weaknesses in the direct exam. If a "beyond the scope" objection is raised to a cross-examination question, the best response probably would be, "Your Honor, R611 allows me to cross on the subject matter of direct examination and "matters affecting the witness's credibility." My cross goes to credibility."

Compound Question.

A compound question has two or more separate questions in a single question, and usually contains the words "and" or "or." A simple "yes" or "no" answer to the question will be unclear. If the witness asked answers "yes" or "no," it is not clear if the "yes" or "no" applies to all the multiple parts of the question or just one part.

Examples:
"On that day, you went shopping <u>and</u> to the beach, didn't you?"
"Did you determine the time of death by interviewing witnesses <u>and</u> by requesting the autopsy report?"
"On that Saturday, did you send the email <u>and</u> also call the banker?"

Cumulative (R403)

Cumulative questions ask for the same information from the same witness multiple times (like asked and answered) or ask multiple witnesses to establish the same facts.

Lack of Foundation (R901)

A lack of foundation objection arises when the lawyer asks a question before establishing the preliminary facts which would permit the questions. The evidence lacks testimony as to its authenticity or source.

Leading Question (R611)
A leading question improperly suggests the answer that the lawyer wants on direct examination. Another test is that the question contains the desired answer. The danger is that the question will make the witness agree with a false suggestion. Often leading questions start with phrases like - "Isn't it true that…" "Did…?" Or ends with "…,right?" Questions that start with the word "So" should be at least a yellow flag that the question might be leading. Although some questions are obviously leading, lawyers and judges often have very different interpretations of what a leading question is. Be prepared to quickly rephrase your question if an objection to it is sustained. Whether or not a question that contains the phrase "whether or not" is leading has been subject to much debate. A lawyer's nonverbal behavior or voice inflection is sometimes considered when determining whether a question is leading.

Leading questions are permissible for preliminary matters, when a party calls a hostile witness or an adverse witness (Rule 611) or when a witness is very young, very old, or mentally challenged. Leading questions are also common and proper on direct examination when laying foundations because under Rule 104 the rules of evidence do not apply, except for privileges, when asking preliminary questions about the admissibility of evidence. Leading questions are also permissible when they are used like a topic sentence in a paragraph to move a witness on direct examination to another part of the scene. For example," Did there come a time when you went into the store?" Of course, the lawyer could get the same result by simply making the statement, "Now I want to ask you some questions about what you did when you went into the store." It is a common belief that the more a lawyer leads on direct examination, the less credibility the witness will have because the witness looks like they are being told what to say during the examination.

Motion to strike
Motions to strike are used two ways. First, Rule of Civil Procedure 12(f) allows for motions to strike certain pleadings. Second, Motions to strike, under evidence R103, are treated similarly to objections and ask the judge to strike inadmissible testimony from the record if the witness has just said the objectionable words. Of course, "striking" is not really striking. The inadmissible words are not removed from the court records but remain in the record even if the testimony is "stricken." The opposing lawyer can ask the judge to instruct the jury to disregard the "stricken" testimony, but psychologically, such an instruction to "disregard" the testimony might highlight the testimony for the jury. Tough choices to make.

Narrative Question, or Calls for A Narrative Answer, or simply Narrative Answer

A narrative objection can refer to a question that asks a witness to tell a story rather than to state only a few specific facts, or refer to witness' answer which is several sentences, or even paragraphs, long. On one hand, narrative answers allow the witness to easily include inadmissible evidence, but on the other hand, a narrative story might more likely provide truthful facts.

Examples of narrative questions:
"What did you do that day?"
"Tell us about the accident."
"Now tell us what everyone said and did at that point."
"What happened that night?"
"How did the accident happen?"
Ans: "First thing I got up and I… Then I went to… After that I … She told me that… And I immediately saw the …"

Non-Responsive Answer: The non-responsive answer objection is made to an answer that does not answer the question that was asked. Simply, the witness does not answer the question asked by the lawyer. The witness is trying to make their own point and take control of the testimony. A problem with nonresponsive answers is that the witness is volunteering information that might be irrelevant or unfairly prejudicial. <u>In theory, only the lawyer asking the question can object to a non-responsive answer</u>. Some judges will only allow this objection from the lawyer who is asking the question. If the objection is sustained, it is often followed by a motion to strike the answer from the record. If the opposing lawyer is considering making a non-responsive answer objection, they are should consider some other appropriate objection such as "irrelevant," "unfairly prejudicial," or "lack of foundation."

Example of a non-responsive answers:
Q: "Did you see the other driver get out of his car right after the accident?"
A: "He told me he had insurance."

Q: "Weren't you the last person the victim saw on the night of his death?"
A: "I had nothing to do with that!"

Speculation – Calls for Speculation – Lack Person Knowledge. (R602)

A speculation objection is proper if the lawyer asks the witness a question that the witness has no personal knowledge about, or the witness testifies about something they have not perceived. A red flag signaling a call for speculation is often a question that starts with, Isn't it possible that…?" A better phrasing to accomplish the same objective would be to focus the question on the witness's personal knowledge and experience by asking for the same information but stating it as follows, "You don't know whether or not…, do you?"

Examples of a question calling for speculation:
"What do you think he was thinking about at that time?"
"Why would she do something like that?"

Vague and Ambiguous Question: Vague and ambiguous questions are asked in ways that are incomprehensible, incomplete, or the answer will be ambiguous. If you, as the opposing lawyer, do not understand the question asked by your opponent, then the witness probably does not understand the question either. Object.

Other Objections

Golden Rule

The Golden Rule objection is made when the opposing counsel places the trier of fact (judge or jury) in the same situation that the case is about.

Examples of a Golden Rule objection:
"Your Honor, what would you have done in a situation like that?"
"Ladies and gentlemen of the jury, would you want someone like that coming into your neighborhood?"

Speaking Objections

A speaking objection is a lawyer's attempt to influence the jury by speaking to the jury by using the objection. Although such objections are very disfavored by judges in jury trials, in nonjury trials such objections can be used to make an argument to the trial judge and influence the decision to be made on the objection.

Examples of speaking objections:
> "Well Judge, I am going to strongly object to this procedure. I feel that I am being sandbagged here and I don't appreciate it."
>
> "Your honor, it doesn't matter what the answer is. Opposing counsel just wants to make a statement. He doesn't care what this witness says,"

Coaching the witness

Such objections can be used to communicate with and coach a witness.

Example of coaching the witness through an objection:
> "Objection. The witness couldn't possibly know that answer."
>> Witness then responds by saying, "I don't know."

Relevance

Questions in a case about some other person, some other event, and some other time, are irrelevant unless the judge find such questions to be relevant in this particular case for a special reason such as to show bias or relevant in this case under Rule 404(b). I call such irrelevant evidence <u>P.E.T. evidence</u> and tell my students that PET evidence is not admissible - evidence about some other Person, or Event, or Time. Furthermore, questions about "**what most people do**" are almost always irrelevant.

Examples of irrelevant "what most people do" objections:
> "<u>Don't most people </u>know that…?"
>
> "Don't most people speed when their car is headed downhill?"

A Few Useful Definitions

Stipulation: Agreement between opposing lawyers to admit certain evidence without the normal in-court proof. The trier of fact then assumes the fact to have been proven.

Offer of Proof:
A statement by a lawyer describing E that the lawyer wants admitted. Proponent summarizes the substance of the excluded evidence to the judge to persuade the judge and to make a record for appeal. – R103

Motion in Limine:
A pre-trial motion seeking a ruling to admit or exclude evidence.

Limited Admissibility:
Evidence can be admitted for one purpose or against one party, but not admitted for another purpose or against another party. – R105

Intrinsic Impeachment - out of the witness' own mouth (almost always) on cross-examination. After a direct exam, the witness is impeached on cross. Almost always permissible.

Extrinsic Impeachment – impeachment coming for the testimony of another witness or the use of a document to impeach. If a witness is not impeached on cross by the opponent's questions, not all types of impeachment are permitted as extrinsic impeachment. The most common limitation is R608(b) – prior bad acts related to dishonestly.

Collateral - relevant only to discredit; does not go to a material matter.

Making and Meeting Objections

A List of Common Possible Objections

Ambiguous	Improper opinion
Argumentative	Improper rehabilitation
Asked and answered	Inadmissible opinion
Assumes facts not in evidence	Incompetent witness
Authentication	Incomplete Inflammatory
Badgering	Insufficient foundation
Best evidence	Irrelevant (Relevance)
Beyond the scope	Lack of foundation
Bias	Lack of personal knowledge
Bolstering	Leading question
Calls for a conclusion	Misleading
Calls for speculation	Misquotes a witness or exhibit
Chain of custody	Misquotes evidence
Collateral	Misstates witness
Competence	More prejudicial than probative
Compound question	Motion to strike
Compromise / Settlement offer	Narrative
Confrontation (lack of)	(Question calls for a narrative)
Confusing	Narrative answer
Counsel is testifying	Non-responsive
Cumulative	Nothing pending
Document speaks for itself	Outside the scope of cross
Expert (Improper opinion)	Overly broad or general
Expert (not qualified)	Parole evidence rule
Habit	Personal knowledge
Harassing the witness	Prejudice (unfair)
Hearsay	Privilege communication
Hypothetical question misused	Relevance
Improper character evidence	Speculation/ Opinion/ Lack of
Improper characterization	personal knowledge
Improper impeachment	Unintelligible
	Vague

There are many more possible objections,
limited only by the lawyer's imagination.

Judges and the local legal culture in your jurisdiction may have other rules or approaches to objections that are not touched on in this handbook. Ask around and learn about them.

Evidentiary Foundations

Foundations - Predicates - Laying the Foundation

Foundations are questions asked by a lawyer to set the groundwork (the foundation) for admitting evidence at trial. The asking of these questions is often referred to as **"laying the foundation"** for the evidence. The word **"predicates,"** when used by trial lawyers, refers to a series of form or sample questions that a lawyer must ask to establish the facts, events, or conditions which are required by the rules of evidence or caselaw before presenting other evidence. Predicates are the questions that are asked when laying the foundation for other evidence. The evidentiary foundation is like the foundation for a building. It provides a solid basis for building up the structure of the case at trial. The necessary foundational questions are not always obvious by reading the rules of evidence.

Foundations may come from local legal culture ("That's the way we do things in this jurisdiction") or from a lawyer or judges prior experience ("That's the way I was taught to do it," or ("That's what I think works best,"), so that's what I am requiring you to do."

Evidentiary Foundations A-17
Foundations – Laying the Foundation - Predicates A-17
Evidentiary Foundations Index...A-18
Bare-Bones Foundations A-20
Admissibility v. Weight A-21
Example of Admissibility and Weight A-21
3 Simple Questions A-22
Steps for Introducing Exhibits...A-23
The Common Evidentiary Foundations...A-25
The Phrases to Move Evidence into a Trial.....................................A-26
Useful Points to Remember..A-27
    Into Evidence A-27
    Make an Offer of Proof..A-27
    Hearsay Within Hearsay A-27
    Public Records Do Not Have to Be Open to The Public A-27
    Compute Generated Record Is Not Hearsay A-27
    Emails Offered to Show Notice, Knowledge or Fear Are Not Hearsay ..A-27
    Demonstrative Evidence A-27
    Chain of Custody A-27
    Distinctive Characteristics A-27
    Authenticate with Personal Knowledge and Distinctive Characteristics.A-28
    Affidavits Are Hearsay and Inadmissible at Trial A-28
    Harrowing A-28
    OTP – Offered to Prove A-28
    Rules Do Not Explain How to Introduce Evidence in Court........A-28
    Laying A Foundation Is Like A Sport A-28
    Mark, Show, Approach, Foundational Questions, Offer A-28
    Magic Words...A-29
    Speak in Generic Terms..A-29
    Publish Means to Show Them Now...A-29
    Chain of Custody Is Only for Fungible Items or Samples to Test A-29
    Basic Tasks A Trial Lawyer Should Be Able to Do A-29
    Best Evidentiary Foundation Resources A-29
Important Evidence Rules to Guide You
    R 103, 104, 901, 612, 613. 801, 803(6), 901, 902(11), 902(13&14),
    105, 106, 1006 ....A-30
Opponent Has the Burden on The Issue of Trustworthiness A-31
Basic Foundation & Impeachment Examples A-32
    Nita Liquor Commission Facts A-33
    Officer Bier's Report A-34
    Diagram of Cut-Rate Liquor Store Area..................................A-35
    Photograph of A Scene A-36
    Diagram of The Scene A-37
    Real Evidence – Thunderbird Wine Bottle..............................A-38

Laying Foundations

- Offering A Contract into Evidence A-39
- Refreshing Memory – Anything A-40
- Writing Used to Refresh Memory – R612 ....A-42
- Refreshing Memory with A Leading Question................................A-43
- Recorded Recollection (Author's Rule)...A-44
- Business Records - Custodian of Records – R803(6)......................A-46
- Business Records Are KRAP...A-47
- Self-Authenticating Business Records Form - Texas A-48
- Demonstrative Evidence - Similar to The Real Item A-49
- Impeachment - Prior Written Inconsistent Statement A-50
- Impeachment by Omission A-52
- Impeachment by Inconsistent Oral Deposition...............................A-54
- Impeachment - Inconsistent Oral Deposition - Short Form...........A-55
- Impeachment - Inconsistent Oral Deposition - Long Form A-56
- Impeachment - Inconsistent Oral Statement A-57
- Learned Treatises Use on Direct Exam – R 803(18) A-58
- 3 Key Points for Using Learned Treatises A-59
- Learned Treatises: Use on Cross – R803(18) A-60
- Voicemail and Phone Conversations A-61

Digital Evidence – Electronically Stored Information – ESI A-63
- A Variety of Different Standards...A-63
- Distinctive Characteristics and Circumstantial Evidence A-65
- Presenting Digital Evidence from A Cell Phone in Court A-66
- Digital Evidence and Self-Authentication A-67

Digital Evidence Foundations A-63
- Email – Outgoing A-68
- Email – Incoming A-69
- Text Message – Received by Witness A-70
- Social Media: Facebook, Instagram, Snapchat, Twitter A-71
- Internet Website – Web Posting A-72
- Fax – Incoming A-73

Foundation for Expert Opinion A-74
Trial Evidence: Cartoon Contest Caption Winners A-78
Negotiation & ADR: Cartoon Contest Caption Winners A-104
History and Restyling of The Federal Rules of Evidence A-109
Teaching Evidence since 4 B.C..A-110
Other Evidence Books in This Series by John Barkai.......................A-111
Dedication..A-113
About the Author..A-113

Bare-Bones Foundations

The foundations provided in this handbook are designed to be brief, what I call "bare-bones foundations." A "bare-bones" foundation uses the minimum necessary questions to admit a piece of evidence or testimony and is less concerned about the "weight" of the evidence to be admitted. Bare-bones foundations are commonly used in non-jury trials. The judge, as trier of fact, should understand the elements of each foundation. On the other hand, what I call "**advocacy foundations**" are more common in jury trials where a jury of laypeople will make the important factual determinations in the case. An advocacy foundation uses much more than the bare minimum number of questions to lay the foundation, with additional questions going to enhance the persuasiveness of the sponsoring witness and the evidence. For example, when using a police officer's report to refresh memory, for recorded recollection, or to impeach, the additional questions might include questions relating to the training or conduct of the officer, such as:

"Did you have training in writing reports?"

"How much training?"

"When you are writing your report, you know that your supervisor will read some of your reports?"

"You know that your future assignments might depend on the quality of your written reports?"

"Do you normally reread your report before submitting it?"

"Do you check your report for accuracy before submitting it?"

Admissibility v. Weight

Foundations are sometimes necessary for evidence to be admissible. As such, they go to the issue of "admissibility," which is about "can" the evidence be included in the trial so that the trier of fact (judge or jury) can consider that evidence in decision-making. On the other hand, the "weight" of evidence is the "value" to be given to the piece of evidence by the trier of fact. Trial judgments are usually determined by which party's admitted evidence is more persuasive, and has the party met the burden of persuasion to the necessary standard (such as: "preponderance of the evidence" or "beyond a reasonable doubt").

Example of Admissibility and Weight

Assume the trial is about a fight. One person says, "He hit me." The other person says, "I did not." Both statements will be admissible, but the trier of fact, after listening to other facts and witnesses, will probably assign different weights or values to the testimony of the two people. Typically, one person will be considered more credible or believable than the other person. The more reliable person's testimony it is said to be given greater weight. It is that weight of the evidence that will eventually lead to a decision for one party or the other. A common statement made by a judge when an opposing party argues against the admissibility of testimony or other evidence is, <u>"That goes to weight, not admissibility."</u> Such a statement by a judge means, "You just lost your battle to exclude that evidence from the trial, but you can still argue that your case is stronger and more persuasive than your opponent's case is."

3 Simple Questions

After handing a physical item to a witness and saying for the record, "Let me show you what has been marked as proposed exhibit number one," the foundation for some physical pieces of evidence can be established with as few as three questions:

> 1) Q: What is it?
>
> 2) Q: How do you know that?
>
> 3) Q: Is it in the same condition as it was on the day of …?"
> (Or, "Is that a fair and accurate representation of the item as it was on …?").

Laying Foundations

Steps for Introducing Exhibits

> **Preliminary steps are:**
> 1) **Have the exhibit marked for identification**
> 2) **Show the proposed exhibit to opposing counsel**
> 3) **Ask permission to approach the witness with the proposed exhibit**

1. **History - How the witness knows the exhibit.**
    Offer some testimony that the witness <u>knows</u> or is <u>familiar with</u> the evidence – such as a document, physical item, photo, diagram, scene, text message, email - or recalls the statement. Even if the witness has only seen the exhibit once before or has just been to the scene shown in the photograph once before, <u>once is enough</u>.

2. **The Litany (a ritualistic repetition of foundational questions)**
    a) Ask the court clerk to **mark the item** (using numbers or letters). The clerk will decide which system to use. In more serious cases in the jurisdiction's higher courts (typically where jury trials are allowed), exhibits are usually required to be marked at least before trial starts, and often during pretrial conferences.
    b) **Show opposing counsel** (this will prevent interruptions) and say, "Let the record reflect that I am showing the defense what has been marked as plaintiff's proposed exhibit number one."
    c) Ask the judge for **permission to approach** the witness. "May I approach the witness?"
    - Q: "**I show you what has been marked as** Plaintiff's (Prosecution's) (Defense's) proposed exhibit # x (or exhibit #x for identification purposes) **and ask whether you can identify it**" (You expect a "yes" answer here.)
    - Q: "What is it?" (They describe it in general terms. "It is the contract/photo of the scene/weapon recovered/drugs seized/diagram of the area/etc.")
    - Q: "How do you know that?" (They answer – "I recognize it. It has my signature on it. / I have been there many times before. / I put my initials on it and the defendant's name/etc.")

Laying Foundations

3. Show Condition or Comparison or Accuracy

Some comparison must be made between the exhibit in court and when the witness became familiar with the exhibit out-of-court. Of the examples that follow, only one such question is necessary.

- "Is this in the **same** condition as when you... [first saw it...seized it...etc.]?"
- "Is this in the **same or substantially** the same condition.... as when you..."   (for item or document)
- "Is it a **fair and accurate representation** of the ... **as it was that day**?"   (for diagram or pictures)
- "**Has it changed** in any significant way?"
- "**How does it compare** to the item you saw that day?"

4. Move or Offer the Exhibit into Evidence

"Your honor, **I offer the exhibit into evidence**." - or, "I move the exhibit into evidence."

You could instead say, "I offer proposed exhibit # 1 into evidence as exhibit # 1," but why make it so confusing? Just say, "I offer the exhibit into evidence."

The judge <u>might</u> ask the opposing counsel, "Any objections?" but the opponent should object immediately after the proponent offers the exhibit, if there is an objection to the admissibility (not the weight). The judge should allow "voir dire" (immediate cross examination limited to the foundation and the admissibility) by the opponent of the exhibit.

The Common Evidentiary Foundations

Physical Items
Photograph (printed)
Diagram of scene
Physical item seized at scene

Common Documents
Refreshing memory
Recorded recollection
Business records in paper
Business records – and self-authentication under R902
Deposition Impeachment (see below)

Records and Treatises
Public record
Learned treatise –
    Use on direct supporting your expert
    Use on cross impeaching their expert

Digital Evidence – from the internet, a cell phone, or a computer
    Also called - ESI – Electronically Stored Information
Emails
Text message – issues of incompleteness
Social Media - Facebook, Instagram, Twitter, Snapchat
Website posting
Voicemail recording
Videos, including on cell phone
Photo on cell phone
Fax
Chatroom conversations

Impeachment
    Impeaching by Prior Written Inconsistent statement
    Impeaching by Omission in Prior Written Statement
    Impeaching by Prior Oral Inconsistent statement
    Impeaching by Inconsistent Oral Deposition Transcript

Phrases to Move Evidence into a Trial

(Pick one and always use it)

"I offer the exhibit into evidence." (By far the easiest to use)

"Your Honor, I ask that what's been previously marked as Plaintiff's Exhibit A for Identification be admitted into evidence as Plaintiff's A."

"At this time, we offer Plaintiff's A for identification into evidence as Plaintiff's exhibit A."

"The Government at this time, would move to introduce Government's Exhibit No. 2 into evidence."

"Your Honor, we'd offer Defense Exhibit B into evidence."

"Your Honor, I move that Plaintiff's Exhibit 3 be introduced into evidence."

"We offer Exhibit A into evidence."

"Your honor, I would like to submit People's exhibit 'A' into evidence."

"We would ask the Court to admit State's Exhibit 4 for Identification as State's 4."

Useful Points to Remember

Offering something "into evidence" means that in a jury trial the exhibit can go into the jury room and be reviewed as many times as the jurors want to look at it.

Make an Offer of Proof – if your evidence is not admitted. R103.

Hearsay within hearsay – statements incorporated into other statements need an additional hearsay exception to be admissible. R805 Hearsay Within Hearsay.

Public records do not have to be "open to the public" but rather are reports and records created by public (government) employees. R803(8)

A record automatically generated by a computer - is not hearsay (computer generated records). No assertion by a person.

Email offered to show notice, knowledge, or fear are not assertions and therefore not hearsay. In a contract or consent form, the words have independent legal significance, which means they operate to form a contract even if they are not true.

Demonstrative evidence – demonstrates or represents some real evidence. Also sometimes called **illustrative evidence**, as compared to **real evidence**, which as some historical connection to the case - such as being the drugs, the gun, etc.

A "chain of custody" is required for fungible items that cannot be identified and distinguished on sight, such as drugs, alcohol, and blood examples - indistinguishable as grains of sand. Often, they are taken into custody and forwarded for laboratory testing. The "chain" makes sure the evidence that is tested is connected to the correct case.

Distinctive characteristics. Evidence tags with initials and case names make items unique and should qualify as a **"Distinctive characteristic"** under R901(b)(4) for authentication purposes.

The most common methods to introduce physical and documentary evidence is **using personal knowledge** and **distinctive characteristics.** R901(b)(1)&(4)

Affidavits are hearsay and not admissible at trial. However, affidavits can be used in summary judgment proceedings if the statements in the affidavits would be admissible in court if testified to by the declarant with personal knowledge. Therefore, lawyers should not be signing affidavits for summary judgement. Potential witnesses with personal knowledge of the facts must sign the affidavits.

HARROWing - a Barkai mnemonic/acronym formed from the first letters of evidence concepts most likely to impact admissibility decisions. Always think of HARROWing when a physical item is going to be introduced, especially if the item is a document or a physical item with words on it. **H**earsay R800s, **A**uthentication R900s, **R**elevance R401, **R**elevance R403, **O**riginal **W**ritings (Best Evidence) R1000s. HARROWing applies to ESI (Electronically Stored Information) such as emails, texts, websites, etc.

OTP - what is the evidence "Offered to Prove?" OTP impacts relevance, admissibility, and the necessary foundation.

The rules of evidence do not tell you how to introduce exhibits although some rules do list the foundational elements which must be included in foundational questions. The hearsay exceptions of Recorded Recollection R803(5) and Records of a Regular Conducted Activity (business records) R803(6) are examples of hearsay exceptions that are so complicated that a novice trial lawyer might want to have the rule in front of them when attempting to lay the foundation.

Laying a foundation is like a sport. Practice before the game.

Steps: Mark/Pre-Mark, Show, Approach, Foundational Questions, Offer
> **Mark exhibits**: 1 day before trial or prior to trial – depending on the court rules.

Magic Words: "<u>in the same or substantially the same condition</u>" or "<u>fair and accurate representation</u>," or "<u>fairly accurate representation</u>," or "<u>fairly represent</u>."

Speak in generic terms when talking about exhibits until the witness identifies the exhibit: "<u>Proposed exhibit # 1</u>" or "<u>Exhibit # 1 for identification purposes</u>," not "Your report," or "Photo of the scene."

To "<u>publish</u>" an exhibit means to show the exhibit to the jury or ask the judge to look at the exhibit now.

Chain of evidence is usually only necessary for fungible items (identical - they all look the same), or items that need testing – drugs, alcohol, blood, DNA. Not every "kink in the link" of the chain of evidence makes evidence inadmissible. Authentication only requires production of evidence "sufficient to support a finding," R901(a)(1), which is a low standard.

Basic tasks that every trial lawyer should be able to do
- introduce documents, physical items, photographs
- refresh memory (almost always done on direct)
- use the recollection recorded hearsay exception (almost always done on direct).
- impeach (almost always done on cross); inconsistent statements & omissions.

The Best Foundation Resources
- Grimm, Joseph & Capra, Best Practices for Authenticating Digital Evidence 69 Baylor L.R. 1 (2017)
- Evidentiary Foundations for Government Attorneys (2015) (from National Attorneys General Training & Research Institute) - (JB: It contains many simple foundations.)
- Edward Imwinkelried, Evidentiary Foundations, (10th ed. 2018) – (The classic source for foundations, but less than you might want about ESI foundations, and more than you might want in the middle of trial.)
- Deanne Siemer, Laying Foundations and Meeting Objections (4th ed. 2013)

Important Evidence Rules to Guide You

R103 - Making an Offer of Proof. – explains how to protect your record if your evidence is excluded.

R104 Preliminary questions.
(a) **Questions of admissibility generally**… In making its determination [the court] is not bound by the Rules of Evidence except those with respect to privileges. [**JB**: meaning <u>you can lead on direct for foundations.</u>]
(b) **Relevancy conditioned on fact.** When the relevancy of evidence depends upon the fulfillment of a condition of fact, the court shall admit it upon, or subject to, the introduction of evidence <u>sufficient to support a finding</u> of the fulfillment of the condition.
   [**JB**: that is a low threshold.]

Rule 901. Requirement of Authentication or Identification
(a) **General provision**. The requirement of authentication or identification as a condition precedent to admissibility is satisfied by <u>evidence sufficient to support a finding</u> that the matter in question is what its proponent claims. [**JB**: <u>that is a low threshold</u>]
(b) **Illustrations.** By way of illustration only…
   (1) **Testimony of witness with knowledge.** Testimony that a matter is what it is claimed to be.
   (4) **Distinctive characteristics and the like.** Appearance, contents, substance, internal patterns, or other <u>distinctive characteristics, taken in conjunction with circumstances.</u>
   (7) **Public records or reports.**
   (9) **Process or system.**

R612 Writing Used to Refresh a Witness's Memory. Witness does not need to be the author. Anything can be used to refresh memory - even "my left shoe" – My in-class example.

R613 Witness's Prior Statement. Impeachment by inconsistent statements and omissions.

R801(d)(1) Not Hearsay: A Declarant-Witness's Prior Statement. (Inconsistent under oath, consistent, or prior ID)

Laying Foundations

R803(6) Records of a Regularly Conducted Activity
(JB: business records are **KRAP)**
(**K**ept in the course, **R**egular practice, **A**t or near the time, **P**ersonal knowledge)

R902 Evidence That Is Self-Authenticating

902(11) Certified Domestic Records of a Regularly Conducted Activity. [Note: There are many certification forms available on the internet.] [Note: Ohio **has adopted** this rule.]

902(13) Certified Records Generated by an Electronic Process or System. [Note: Ohio **has adopted** this rule.]

902(14) Certified Data Copied from an Electronic Device, Storage Medium, or File. [Note: Ohio **has adopted** this rule.]

R105 Limited Admissibility (admitted against only one party or for a limited purpose)

R106 Remainder of / related writing [JB: admit now]

R1006 Summaries...voluminous writings which cannot conveniently be examined in court.

The Opponent Has the Burden
On the Issue of Trustworthiness of Records

Burden of showing a record lacks trustworthiness is on the opponent in the Federal rules - R803(6)(7)(8) ..."and, the opponent does not show ...a lack of trustworthiness."

Note: **Ohio NOT has adopted** these burden rules

Basic Foundations & Impeachment Examples

Several of the following foundation and impeachment examples are based upon the facts of

Nita Liquor Commission v. Cut-Rate Liquor and Jones*

In this famous, fictional case from NITA (National Institute of Trial Advocacy), Walter Watkins was observed going into the Cut-Rate Liquor Store by Officer Bier and his partner from their unmarked car which was parked across the street from the liquor store. The officers had a partial view into the store and saw Watkins appear to purchase liquor at the counter. Watkins was arrested outside the store as he was leaving with a brown paper bag which contained a bottle of Thunderbird Wine. Cut-Rate Liquors and the clerk Dan Jones were issued citations for selling liquor to a person under the influence of liquor.

* This NITA Liquor Problem is used with the permission of the National Institute of Trial Advocacy (NITA). The terms "Officer Bier, Thunderbird Wine, Jackson & 7th Street, April 5th, Walter Watkins, and shoulders up" used in this publication are original to the Nita Liquor Commission v. Cut-Rate Liquor and Jones problem from *Problems in Trial Advocacy* by Donald H. Beskind and Anthony J. Bocchino, published by the National Institute of Trial Advocacy. The basis of the NITA Liquor problem and the specified terms are used here with permission.

NITA Liquor Commission
v.
Jones

The Facts

This case is a civil action brought by the Liquor Commission against Dan Jones and the Cut-Rate Liquor Store, for civil penalties, including possible revocation of Cut-Rate's liquor license. Investigator Bier is a typical investigator-police officer and has investigated many such incidents. Bier's official report appears on the next page along with a diagram of the scene.

Dan Jones and the Cut-Rate Liquor Store deny that Watkins was intoxicated on the evening of April 5 when he was in their store. Jones says that Watkins did not appear to be intoxicated when he observed Watkins in the store. Watkins was convicted of public intoxication at a prior trial. Watkins is not present for this Cut-Rate case.

1. Prepare to do a direct examination of Officer Bier for the government.

2. Prepare to do a cross examination of Officer Bier for the Defense.

Officer Bier's Report

NITA LIQUOR COMMISSION OFFICIAL REPORT

My partner Donald Smith and I are investigators for the Nita Liquor Commission. On the evening of April 5, at approximately 8:45 p.m., we were parked near the Cut-Rate Liquor Store when we observed an individual, later identified as Walter Watkins, attempting to cross 7th Street. Mr. Watkins was staggering and had great difficulty making it to the other side of the street. He stumbled and almost fell at the curb on the south side of 7th Street. He walked to the entrance of the Cut-Rate Liquor Store, and then paused for a few moments before he entered the store. The front of the store had a plate glass window with displays and advertising in it. From our car, we could see Mr. Watkins from the shoulders up through the window. We observed Mr. Watkins approach the counter and say a few words to the clerk, Dan Jones. A few minutes later, Watkins emerged from the store carrying a bottle of Thunderbird wine in a brown paper sack.

I stopped Mr. Watkins as he exited the store. I detected the odor of alcohol and administered a field sobriety test. I then arrested Watkins and issued him a citation for public intoxication, seized the wine, and issued a citation to Dan Jones and the Cut-Rate Liquor store for violation of H.R.S. 281-78 which contains the following language:

> No licensee nor its employees shall sell or furnish any liquor to any person at the time under the influence of liquor.

I have attached a diagram of the scene to this report.

Date: April 5   Time: 22:15

signed J. Bier

_____

Diagram of Cut-Rate Liquor Store Area

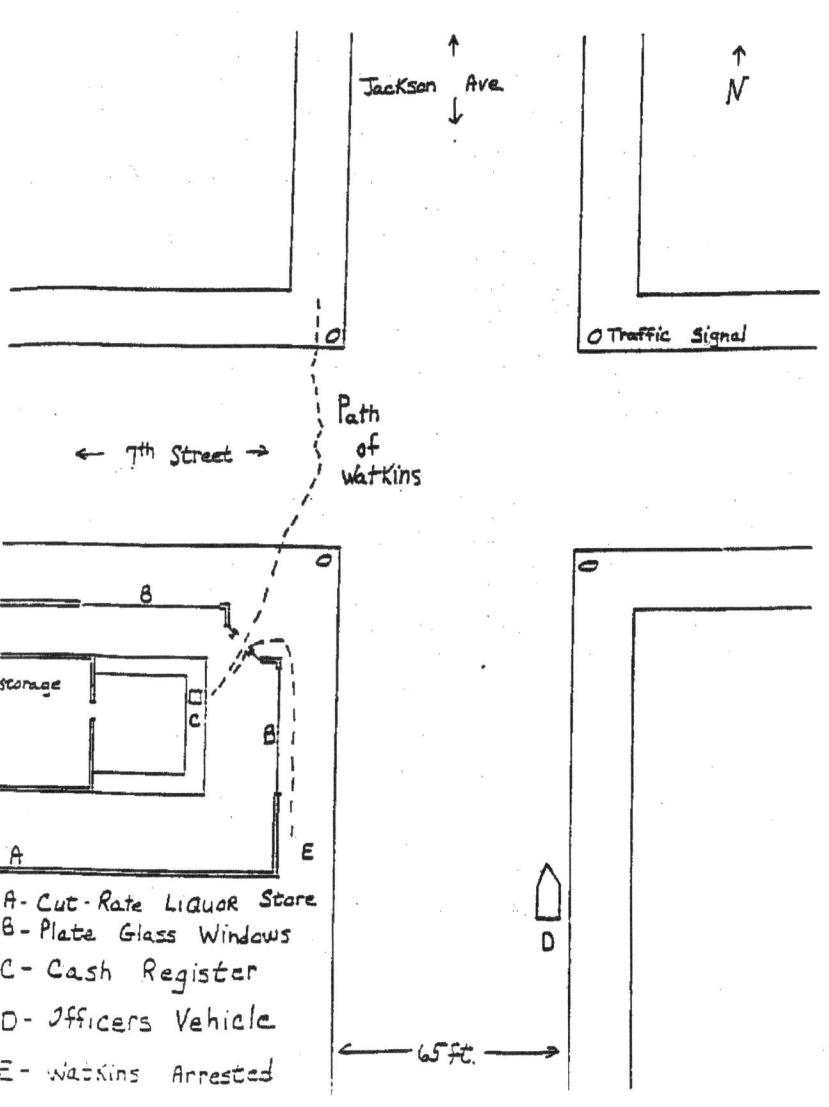

Laying Foundations

Photograph of a Scene

Introduce a photograph of Cut-Rate Liquor Store where the clerk and the liquor store were charged with selling liquor to an intoxicated person. R901(B)(1) (Testimony of a Witness with Knowledge)

Q: Officer Bier, where were you on the night of April 5?
A: Parked in an unmark car outside Cut-Rate Liquor Store.

Q: Let me show you what has been marked as Plaintiff's proposed exhibit # 1.   <u>What is it?</u>
A: It is a photograph of Cut-Rate Liquor Store where I was parked on April 5th.

Q: <u>How do you know that?</u>
A: I was at the store that night. I recognize it. I took the photo.

Q: Is the photograph a <u>fair and accurate representation</u> of Cut-Rate Liquor store as it appeared <u>on April 5th</u>?
A: Yes.

Q: Your Honor, I offer the exhibit into evidence.

Enhancements/Additional Questions
 - "Please describe the appearance of the store."
 - "How many times have you seen the Cut-Rate Liquor Store?" (Ask this question only if the witness has been to the store many times. However, being there once is enough for the foundation.) The witness can authenticate the photo even if the trial event was the only time the witness ever saw the store pictured in the photo

Additional Points:
 - The photographer is not a necessary witness.
 - The witness's personal knowledge of the contents of the photograph is all that is necessary.
 - The witness does not have to have seen the photograph before coming to court.
 - Print the photo and bring copies to court for the judge, jury, and opposing counsel.
 - The photo could be a "Street view" from Google Maps that the witness has never seen before.

Diagram of the Scene

Demonstrative Evidence

Diagram from Officer Bier's Report

After some testimony about the events.

Q: Officer Bier, did you make a diagram of the scene that night? (Ans: Yes)

Q: Let me show you what has been marked as Plaintiff's proposed exhibit # 1. <u>What is it?</u> (Ans: My diagram)

Q: <u>How do you know that?</u> (Ans: I drew it. I remember it. That's my writing)

Q: Is it a <u>fair and accurate representation</u> of the intersection of Jackson and 7th Streets <u>on April 5th</u>? (Ans: Yes.)

Q: Is the proposed exhibit in the <u>same condition</u> as it was when you drew it on April 5th? (Ans: Yes.)

Q: Your Honor, I offer the exhibit into evidence.

Real Evidence

The Bottle of Thunderbird Wine Seized by Officer Bier

After some testimony about the events.

Q: Officer Bier, <u>what, if anything, did you recover</u> from Mr. Watkins that night?
(Ans: A bottle and a bag)

Q: Let me hand you what has been marked as Plaintiff's proposed exhibit # 2. <u>What is it?</u>
(Ans: The bottle and bag I seized from Watkins)

[If the bottle is in a bag, leave it in the bag. Have both the bottle and bag marked separately, e.g., Exhibits 1 and 2, A and B, 1 and 1A. Let the witness take the bottle out of the bag, like unwrapping a present. It will create some interest in what might be an otherwise boring trial.]

Q: <u>How do you know that?</u>
[Ans: My initials, in my handwriting, are on the bag along with the words "Cut-Rate Liquor" and "April 5."]

Q: Is the proposed exhibit # 2 <u>in the same or substantially the same condition</u> as it was when you recovered it from Watkins on April 5th?
(Ans: Generally, yes. However, some of the liquid was removed for testing for alcohol.)

Q: Your Honor, I offer the exhibit into evidence.

Offering A Contract into Evidence

Q: Mr. Johnny, I now want to ask you some questions about your dealings with Mr. King. In September, two years ago, did you have several conversations with Mr. King?
A: Yes. I did.

Q: What was the result of those conversations?
A: Mr. King and I entered into a contract for legal work.

Assume the exhibit has been pre-<u>marked</u> before the day of trial

Q: Let the record reflect that I am <u>handing</u> Mr. Johnny what has been pre-marked, as required by Court Rule, Plaintiff's proposed Exhibit # 1.
<u>What is it Mr. Johnny?</u>
A: It's the contract between me and Mr. King for the legal work that I was going to do for him.

Q: <u>How do you know that?</u> [Prepare the witness to answer this question]
A: I drafted this contract. I recognize it. That's my signature on it as well as Mr. King's.

Q: Is the contract in the <u>same condition</u> as it was two years when you both signed it.
A: Yes. There are no alterations to the contract.

Q: You Honor, I <u>offer</u> the exhibit into evidence

Laying Foundations

Refreshing Memory
(Anything can be used to refresh memory)

<u>Refreshing memory is almost always done on direct examination. Impeachment is almost always done on cross examination.</u>

In the NITA case, assume witness Bier forgets some of Mr. Watkin's movements on the street. Refresh Bier's memory from his report. R612.

Q: Please describe Watkin's movements as he crossed 7th Street.
A: He staggered and had great difficulty getting to the other side of the street.

Q: Do you recall anything else about Watkins as he crossed the street.
A: Not really

Q: Officer Bier <u>did you make a report</u> in this case? A: Yes.

Q: Let me hand you what has been marked as Plaintiff's proposed exhibit # 3. <u>What is it?</u>
[Note: You are not going to introduce the document. Some judges might allow you to refresh memory without marking the exhibit, but the better practice is to have the document marked.]
A: My report.

Q: Please <u>read it to yourself</u>, especially the 4th and 5th lines.
    (Note: You can focus the witness on what you want to witness to pay attention to.)

Q: <u>Let the record reflect that I am taking proposed exhibit # 3 away</u> from the Officer.
Now Officer Bier, is your memory refreshed?
A: Yes.

Q: What else do you now recall about how Watkins crossed 7th Street?
A: Watkins stumbled as he crossed 7th Street
        (Discussion continued on the next page)

Recommendation: I suggest that you do not ask the witness, "Would anything refresh your memory." Just start refreshing. Isn't it strange to say, "Witness, I know you cannot remember, but can you remember anything that would help you remember what you have already forgotten?" Just refresh.

Additional points: The document used to refresh is not introduced into evidence. The witness' memory was refreshed. There is no need to introduce the document. There is no hearsay issue.

Writing Used to Refresh Memory

If a writing was used to refresh memory, R612 allows

> as a matter of right, if the document was used in court;
> with judge's discretion, if the document was used out of court

the opponent to:

1) see the writing in court,
2) inspect it
3) cross-examine on it, and
4) introduce portions of it (related to the testimony)

Simply: **Get, Inspect, Cross, Introduce.**

However, it would be very unusual for an opponent to introduce the document because most of the document would hurt the opponent's case. If the opponent wanted to introduce only portions of the document, the lawyer who used it to refresh memory would have an argument that under R106, in fairness other parts of the document should be considered at the same time.

Rule 612. Writing used to refresh memory. (paraphrased)
If a witness uses a writing to refresh memory for the purpose of testifying, either:
 (1) while testifying; or
 (2) before testifying, if the court in its discretion determines it is necessary in the interests of justice,
an adverse party is entitled
to have the writing produced at the hearing,
to inspect it,
to cross-examine the witness thereon, and
to introduce in evidence those portions which relate to the testimony of the witness.

Refreshing Memory with a Leading Question

(Using the same facts as the previous example)

Q: Do you recall anything else about Watkins as he crossed the street.
A: Not really

Q: Did he stumble and almost fall?

Opposing Lawyer: Objection: Leading

Q: I'll rephrase my question. What else do you recall about Watkins as he crossed the street.
A: Now I recall that he did stumble and almost fell crossing the street. I'm nervous. I forgot.

Note: The witness's credibility might have decreased somewhat because of the leading question, but the lawyer got the answer that was needed. The less important the information, the more likely leading will have little or no impact on your case.

Leading on Minor Issues When the Witness Has Gone Off Course

Q: What day of the week did this happen?
A: Tuesday.

Q: You said Tuesday. Did you actually mean Monday?
A: Oh right, sorry. It was Monday.

Recorded Recollection (Author's Rule)

Recorded recollection is a hearsay exception that allows <u>for reading into evidence</u> a statement that was made by a witness on the stand who can no longer recall the facts even after there has been attempts to refresh the witness's memory. Recorded recollection is <u>almost always done on direct examination</u> with a witness the lawyer has called to testify. This foundation is complicated and not intuitive.

In the NITA problem, assume that attempts to refresh the witness's memory did not work. Therefore, assume the previous question and answer were:

Q: What else do you now recall?
A: Sorry, I truly do not remember any more.

[Lawyer now moves into the foundation for Recorded Recollection, under R803(5).

Q: Let me again show you proposed exhibit # 3. That is your report of this incident, right? [Note: Leading is appropriate when establishing any foundations under R 104] (a)).
A: Yes

Q: You made that report when the incident was <u>fresh</u> in your mind?
A: Yes, just about an hour after the incident.

Q: Does the report <u>accurately reflect your knowledge</u> of the incident at the time of the incident?
A: Yes.

Q: Although you <u>once knew the details</u> of the incident and wrote them in your report, right now <u>you cannot now recall</u> the details of the incident well enough <u>to testify fully and accurately</u>, right?
A: Yes.

Q: Your honor, I would now <u>like to read</u> into the record those parts of the report that the witness no longer remembers. [Or, you could ask to have the witness read the portions of the report.]

(Discussion continued on the next page)

RULE 803(5) Recorded recollection. A memorandum or record concerning a matter about which a witness once had knowledge but now has insufficient recollection to enable the witness to testify fully and accurately, shown to have been made or adopted by the witness when the matter was fresh in the witness' memory and to reflect that knowledge correctly. If admitted, the memorandum or record may be read into evidence but may not itself be received as an exhibit unless offered by an adverse party.

Additional Points: "Admission" into evidence comes from reading parts of the document into evidence. The document is not physically admitted by the proponent of the evidence. It cannot be taken into the jury room. Information in this hearsay document is admitted (heard) only once like oral testimony.

Almost always, the witness was the author of the document used as the recorded recollection. Refreshing memory under R612 and recorded recollection are almost always done on direct examination. Witnesses are impeached on cross, not refreshed. You would not normally use recorded recollection on cross because almost all of the document goes against your client.

I think most lawyers prefer to read the recollection on direct examination themselves and not have the witness do it. By reading the recollection yourself, you can add what you consider the best tone, volume, pace, and emphasis for your case. Remember, when you use a past recollection recorded with your witness on direct, you cannot physically introduce the document into evidence. The proponent of the past recollection recorded "admits" the recollection by reading it, not physically admitting it.

Recorded recollection documents are not business records. Business records do get admitted into evidence. The difference is that if admitted, the evidence can be taken into the jury room and be consulted by the jury many times during deliberations.

A past recollection recorded includes all notes that a witness makes on any type of document. In evidence class, I pull out my wallet and show students all the recorded recollections that I have in my wallet (post-it notes, notes on business cards, notes on little scraps of paper, etc.) and any notes I have taken on my cell phone. Recorded Recollections is a hearsay document which can only be read into evidence but not physically introduced, at least not by the proponent of a recorded recollection.

Business Records - Custodian of Records
(The actual hearsay exception is for "Regularly Conducted Activity," but is usually called "Business Records")

To prove that Cut-Rate Liquors had Thunderbird Wine in stock on April 5, a business record can be offered.

Q: Please state your name, occupation, and why you are here today.
A: I am Mr. Data, an employee of Cut-Rate Liquors. My duties at Cut-Rate include serving as the custodian of business inventory records for Cut-rate. I am here today pursuant to a subpoena to bring inventory records of Cut-Rate for April 5th.

Q: Did you bring with you today a copy of the Cut-Rate inventory records pertaining to Thunderbird wine for April 5th with you?
A: Yes.

Q: Do you know how Cut-Rate maintains its inventory records?
A: Yes.

Q: I show you what has been pre-marked as proposed exhibit # 1 and ask if you can identify what it is?
A: Yes, I can. Those are the Cute-Rate inventory records that I brought to court.

Q: Are those inventory records made by a person with <u>personal knowledge</u>, <u>at or near the time</u> the inventory is taken?
A: Yes.

Q: Are those records <u>kept in the course of a regularly conducted activity</u> of a business?
A: Yes.

Q: Is making those records a <u>regular practice</u> of Cut-Rate's business?
A: Yes.

Q: Your Honor, I offer the exhibit into evidence.

Publishing a Business Record: After being admitted, the business record can be "published" (which means it can be shown to the trier to fact). Depending on the judge's practice, the lawyer might be able to have the information from the record read to jury when it is admitted. If so, the Q & A could be:

Q: What do those records say about whether Cut-Rate had Thunderbird Wine in stock on April 5th?
A: "Thunderbird Wine, quantity 5," which means that Cut-Rate had five bottles of Thunderbird Wine in stock on April 5.

Remember, **business records are KRAP**. That acronym always gets my students' attention, and it helps them remember the foundation's components. **KRAP** – means:
Kept in the course,
Regular practice,
At or near the time,
Personal knowledge

The **custodian of records or other qualified witness** required by the business record evidence rule is often the owner of the business, a bookkeeper, or anybody who works in the business. They just have to be able to answer questions to provide the appropriate foundation.

Although it adds to the weight of the evidence to have a witness who has been employed for many years in the data collection of the business, that is not required. The custodian only needs to be able to testify to the foundation requirements. The custodian could have only been the custodian for one day, if they can credibly answer the foundational questions (although that fact might go to the weight of the evidence, but not its admissibility). The custodian does not have to be employed on the day the record was made.

I would prefer to use a self-authenticating business record. The custodian is open to a difficult cross.
"Do you know who made the business entry?" – Know their work history? Have they been disciplined? Know their accuracy? Are they still with the company? (Of course, you need a good faith basis).

Self-Authenticating Business Records

The Federal Rules of Evidence were amended in 2002 to allow business records to be self-authenticated by a written certification of the custodian or other qualified witness, which means that a witness does not have to appear in court. R902(11)(12). Many states have created statutes or forms to be used for the certification. An example of such a certification affidavit follows and many are available on the internet.

TEXAS FORM

Business Records Affidavit

FORM AR-1(08/10) | Tax Year | HCAD Account Number

This affidavit should be executed before a Notary Public or other official authorized to administer oaths and attached to the applicable business records. Please print or type.

Before me, the undersigned authority, personally appeared _____, who being by me duly sworn, deposed as follows:

My name is _____, I am of sound mind, capable of making this affidavit, and personally acquainted with the facts herein stated:

I am the custodian of the records of _____. Attached hereto are
(NAME OF BUSINESS)
_____ pages of records from _____. These
(NAME OF BUSINESS)
said _____ pages of records are kept by _____
(NAME OF BUSINESS)
in the regular course of business, and it was the regular practice of said entity for an employee or representative with knowledge of the act, event, condition, opinion, or diagnosis, recorded to make the record or to transmit information thereof to be included in such record; and the record was made at or near the time or reasonably soon thereafter. The records attached hereto are the original or exact duplicates of the original.

_____
Affiant's Signature

SWORN TO AND SUBSCRIBED before me on the _____ day of _____.

(seal)

_____
Notary Public, State of Texas

_____
Notary's Printed Name

_____
My commission expires

Demonstrative Evidence Similar to the Real Item

Assume the bottle of Thunderbird wine in the Nita Liquor Commission case was dropped and broken after the contents had been tested in the lab and showed that it contained alcohol. At trial, a lawyer wants to introduce a bottle similar to the actual bottle of Thunderbird wine.

Q: Officer Bier, do you recognize proposed exhibit # 5?
A: Yes. I do.

Q: What is it?
A: It is a bottle like the one sold by Cut-Rate on the night of the incident.

Q: How do you know that?
A: I am a Liquor Commission Investigator. I am very familiar with Thunderbird wine as part of my job.

Q: "Is this bottle similar to the bottle you seized from Watkins on April 5?"
A: Yes.

Q: I offer the exhibit into evidence.

If there is a relevance objection to the "similar" bottle, the lawyer examining the witness needs to be ready to say, "Your honor, this bottle is relevant to show ...[some appropriate statement]." For example, the size and weight of the bottle suggests that Mr. Watkins could not have smuggled the bottle into the liquor store under his clothing. The similar bottle is not offered as the bottle that was sold that night, but it is being offered to prove something else, which is an example of limited admissibility under R105. The lawyer should not say, although it might be true, "My evidence professor always told us to introduce some physical evidence into the trial to wake up the trier of fact." [Such a statement offers a good trial strategy, but not a good response to the judge's question about relevance.]

Impeachment by Prior Written Inconsistent Statement
R613

Impeach Officer Bier from his report in the NITA problem, assuming Bier testified on direct exam, "I saw Watkins from the waist up inside the store."

> Direct exam testimony was "...from the <u>waist</u> up...."
> Report says "...from the <u>shoulders</u> up..."

Q: T<u>oday</u> you testified on direct examination[1] that you could see Watkins inside the store from the <u>waist up</u>? (said in a disbelieving tone) (Commit to today's testimony.)
A: Yes.

Q: You made a written report in this case within a few hours of the incident? (Credit prior statement's reliability)
A: Yes.

Q: Let the record reflect that I am handing the witness proposed exhibit #x. Mr. Bier, proposed exhibit #x is the report you made within a couple of hours after the incident?
A: Yes.

Q: That is your signature on the report?
A: Yes

Q: Even though you said on direct examination that you could see Mr. Watkins inside the store from the waist up, doesn't it say right here in your report (pointing to it) that "we could see Mr. Watkins from the <u>shoulders up</u> through the window"?
A: Yes.

(Discussion continued on the next page)

---

[1] I suggest that you only use the phrase – "You testified on direct" – when you are going to impeach a witness with a prior statement. Do not use that phrase when you are asking questions about a real event that took place in your case. What happened on the day of the incident might be different that what a witness testified to on direct. You should keep the trier of fact's attention on the incident itself, not the testimony on direct – unless you are impeaching that direct testimony.

Stop. Ask no further questions on this topic. Don't say, "Are you lying today or were you lying then?" Such a question is probably argumentative and objectionable anyway. Do not argue with the witness or ask the witness to admit they are not telling the truth. Save the credibility argument for closing argument. In closing argument, you can make an argument without having the witness trying to explain away your impeachment.

Understand the difference between testimony about "waist up" and "shoulders up." If Officer Bier could see Mr. Watkins inside the store from the waist up, he could have seen the bottle of wine, the cash register, any money changing hands, and the wine bottle changing hands. All those facts go to showing that there was a sale of wine in violation of the statute. However, if the officer could only see inside the store at the shoulders up level, then he was not able to see any direct sale and the defense has a better argument.

Three impeaching steps here: commit; credit; and confront. 1) <u>Commit</u> the witness to the statement made on direct, 2) <u>credit</u> the prior out-of-court statement, and 3) <u>confront</u> the witness with the difference.

<u>By putting the conflicting statements in one sentence by using a dependent clause</u> ("Even though you said on direct examination that…"), <u>the trier of fact cannot miss the contradiction.</u> Some impeaching lawyers will emphasize certain words in their questions, so the trier of fact does not miss the inconsistency. For example, they would emphasize with tone, volume, pace, and any other nonverbal's, the words "waist up" and "shoulder up." The impeaching lawyer might want to make eye contact with the judge or the jury when emphasizing those words.

Additional questions that are sometimes asked, especially if it is a jury trial:
    Your prior statement was made closer in time to the event than your statement today?
    Your memory was better at the earlier time?
    You have had training on how to write reports?
    You know that your supervisor will read your reports?
    You know that you are evaluated on, and perhaps even promoted or demoted based on the quality of your reports?

Impeachment by Omission

Assume that <u>Bier testified on direct exam,</u> "As I was sitting in my car watching Watkins <u>inside the store, I saw that Watkins stumble and almost fall as he approached the counter.</u>" However, Officer Bier's report does not say that Watkins stumbled and almost fell inside the store. In fact, the report indicates that the officer could only see Watkins from the shoulders up as he approached the counter. Impeachment by omission - meaning that the witness testified in court to something that was not in the report - it is a little harder to accomplish than a direct prior inconsistent statement, but it is still very doable.

Q: <u>You testified on direct</u> examination that you saw Mr. Watkins stumble and almost fall as he approached the counter inside from the store? (Credit prior statement's reliability)
A: Yes.

Q: You made a written report in this case within an hour of the incident, right?
A: Yes.

Q: I am handing the witness proposed exhibit #x.
This is the report you made within a couple of hours after the incident, isn't it?
A: Yes.

Q: That is your signature on the report, isn't that true?
A: Yes

Q: <u>Even though you said on direct examination</u> that you saw Mr. Watkins <u>stumble and almost fall</u> as he approached the counter <u>inside</u> the store, <u>nowhere</u> in this report that you prepared <u>does it state</u> that you saw Watkins stumble and almost fall <u>inside</u> the store, does it? [If the witness takes time to look for it in the report, give them as much time as they want to take.
A: No, it doesn't say that.

The report says nothing about Watkins' behavior in the store. Behavior in the store is critical to proving that defendant Jones knew that Watkins was intoxicated.

Additional questions beyond the bare-bones foundation.
Lawyer could build up the report, for example:

> "You try to put everything that is important in the report, right?"
> "They taught you to do that in the department training, right?"

The potential re-direct examination:
If it were my witness who was impeached, my redirect would go something like this:

Q: Officer, how do you explain what seems to be an inconsistency between your direct testimony that Watkins stumbled inside the store and your report, which does not mention Watkins stumbled inside the store?

A: [Perhaps the best answer would be] I can't put everything into the report. But I clearly remember that he stumbled inside the store.

Impeachment by Inconsistent Oral Deposition

Assume the same factual inconsistency of testimony on direct examination that Mr. Watkins stumbled inside the store, but this time also assume that Officer Bier gave an oral deposition under oath and gave an answer that did not mention any stumbling inside the store.

After laying a foundation which would include the procedures involved in the deposition, such as:
- You came to my office?
- You took an oath to tell the truth?
- I told you that if you didn't understand the question, you should tell me you don't understand?
- You had an opportunity to review and correct the transcript some weeks after the deposition?
- After you read the typed deposition, you signed the deposition as being accurate?

then complete the impeachment by reading the questions that were asked and the answers that were given at the deposition.

The impeaching sequence could go something like this:

Q: Even though you said on direct that Watkins stumbled and almost fell in the store when he was at the counter, at your deposition weren't you asked this question, and didn't you give this answer:

> Q: Now Officer Bier, how was Watkins walking when he was inside the store?
> A: I can't say for sure. My view into the store was obstructed.

A: Yes, that is what it says.

You want to confine your questions to what the witness said at the deposition, not what the witness remembers now. Your opponent will no doubt do redirect examination to try to rehabilitate the witness.

Impeachment by Inconsistent Oral Deposition - Short Form

On direct examination, the witness said, "The light was green." You want to impeach with the witness' deposition that says, "The light was red."

Q: On direct examination you said the light was green?
A: Yes.

Q: Even though on direct examination you said that the light was green, at the deposition weren't you asked the following question, and didn't you give the following answer?
    Q: What color was the light?
    A: The light was red.
A: Yes.

Laying Foundations

Impeachment by Inconsistent Oral Deposition - Long Form

On direct examination, the witness said, "The light was green." You want to impeach with the witness' deposition that says, "The light was red."

Highlight the Inconsistency
Q. On direct examination you said the light was green. [A: Yes]
Q.   There is no question in your mind about that? [A: No question.]

Lock the Witness into The Testimony (you can omit this step)
Q.   Have you ever said anything different? [No]
Q.   Are you sure it was green? [Yes]
Q.   Isn't it true that the light was in fact red? [No]

Build Up the Impeaching Document
Q. You remember coming to my office last year to answer some questions?
Q. You came for a deposition on July 11, last year?
Q. I asked you questions, and you gave me answers, isn't that right?
Q. Your lawyer sat next to you while you answered?
Q. A court reporter took down your answers?
Q. That reporter gave you an oath to tell the truth?
Q. You agreed to tell the truth?
Q. After that deposition, the Q's and A's were typed up and you had a chance to read it over?
Q. After making sure it was correct, you signed it didn't you?
Q. This is your signature, isn't it?
Q. This deposition was just four months after the accident?
Q. Even though on direct examination you said that the light was green, at the deposition weren't you asked the following question, and didn't you give the following answer?
   Q: What color was the light?
   A: The light was red.

Impeachment by Inconsistent Oral Statement
(Assuming only the cross-examining lawyer heard the inconsistent statement)

Assume that although Bier testified on direct exam that "Watkins stumbled and almost fell inside the store," Bier was overheard outside the courtroom say to a person who is not available to testify, "I never really saw Watkins stumble inside the store." However, only the lawyer for Cut-Rate Liquor heard Bier's statement.

This is an inconsistent oral statement. Unlike most inconsistent statements, this one was <u>not made prior</u> to the in-court testimony on direct exam. <u>This statement was made after</u> the in-court testimony.

This fact pattern presents a special problem if the lawyer was the only person who overhead the statement. If Bier denies making the statement, the cross-examiner does not have a witness who could be called to the stand to complete the impeachment of Bier. So, if no one other that the lawyer overhead the statement, what can the lawyer do? The lawyer certainly cannot testify in this case.

A suggestion would be to handle this problem by being as detailed as possible during the questioning leading up to the impeaching question. If the trier of fact believes the details, the trier of fact might believe that Bier also made the final statement ("I never saw him stumble inside the store.").

Detailed questioning
Q: During the break, you went outside the courtroom, didn't you?
Q: And you sat on the bench outside?
Q: You sat next to a man wearing a blue shirt, right?
Q: And the two of you had a conversation?
Q: You talked for about 5 minutes, right?
Q: "Even though you said on direct exam in court just 30 minutes ago that Watkins stumbled and almost fell in the store when he was at the counter, didn't you say to a man on a bench outside this courtroom just 10 minutes ago, "I never really saw Watkins stumble inside the store?"

Learned Treatises:
Use on Direct Exam to Support Your Expert
R 803(18) – Hearsay Exception

After an expert testifies that it is not possible to determine if the plaintiff's epileptic seizures are caused by the plaintiff's auto accident, the following questioning takes place to use a learned treatise to support the expert's opinion. This is an example of using a "paper expert," or said another way, getting the opinion of two experts but only calling one as a witness.

Q: Dr. Rosenberg, are you familiar with the text called Medicine written by Dr. Mark Fishman?
A: Yes

Q: Let me show you proposed exhibit #1. What is it?
A: It is the book called Medicine written by Dr. Mark Fishman.

Q: Is it a recognized as a reliable authority in the field of medicine?
A: Yes

Q: What does the Fishman text say about the causes of epileptic seizures?
A: On page 135, Fishman says that a cause is found for seizures in less than 25% of the cases.

Additional questions might be:

Q: Does the learned treatise (the text) support or contradict your opinion?

Q: What do you make of this information.

Using a learned treatise as a hearsay exception can <u>only done by reading</u> the treatise to the trier of fact, but <u>not by physically introducing</u> the treatise into evidence. FRE 803(18)

3 Key Points for Using the Learned Treatise

To use a learned treatise on either direct or cross-examination,
1) there must be an expert <u>on the witness stand</u>,
2) the treatise has been established as a <u>reliable authority</u>, and
3) the statement may be <u>only read</u> into the record, but the treatise cannot be physically introduced into evidence.

Learned Treatises: Use on Cross to Impeach the Opposing Expert

After establishing that Mark Fishman's text called "Medicine" is a reliable authority in the field of medicine, either by your expert, or by your opponent's expert, or by judicial notice (Note: judges seldom take judicial notice on this subject), the lawyer below uses the learned treatise on cross examination to contradict the opposing party's expert witness. A statement in a treatise can be used to impeach the opponent's expert and as substantive evidence (meaning for the truth of the statement – this is a hearsay exception).

Q: Dr. Barron, you testified during your direct examination that Mr. Fulbright's epilepsy was caused by the auto accident, right?
A: Yes.

Q: Dr., there is no medical evidence that Mr. Fulbright showed any clinical evidence of brain injury immediately after the incident is there?
A: That's correct.

Q: And no evidence of a skull fracture?
A: That's also correct.

Q: And no evidence of bloody spinal fluid, right?
A: Correct again.

Q: Dr., doesn't the text called, Medicine, written by Mark Fishman, indicate on page 132 that the four symptoms most commonly found with epileptic seizures are 1) loss of consciousness, 2) clinical evidence of brain injury immediately after the incident, 3) skull fracture, and 4) bloody spinal fluid?
A: Yeah, Fishman does say that.

Q: Your Honor, no further questions.

Voicemail, Phone Conversations, Recorded Phone Conversations

There is nothing special about the identification of a telephone call. Authentication for voice identification is covered in the R901(b)(5)&(6).

Do you know X?

How do you know X?

How long have you known X?

Have you ever spoken with X on the phone?

How often have you spoken with X on the phone?

On [the day in question] did you have a phone conversation with X?

Who initiated that call?

[If **your** witness initiated the call]

> How did you make the call? [Ans: used contacts list on cell phone; used recent call list on cell phone; used landline]
>
> Was their name already in your cell phone from previous calls to them?
>
> Did you recognize the voice when your call was answered?
>
> Who were you talking to?

(Continued on next page)

[If the **other party** initiated the call]

>   Could you tell who was calling you?
>
>   How could you tell who was calling you? [Name appeared on my cell phone]
>
>   Why did their name appear in your cell phone? [I had name in my contacts list from many previous calls]
>
>   Who was on the phone when you answered the call? [The defendant]
>
>   How did you know that? [We have talked many times before. I recognized his voice.]

What did he say during that call?

Digital Evidence
Electronically Stored Information – ESI

Electronically Stored Information (EIS) includes emails, text messages, websites, fax, social media, computer printouts, and other digital records. Although we evidence professors will tell you that the classic rules of evidence, created before cell phones, computers, and the Internet, are more than adequate for the new digital world, some people doubt it.

Yet truly, introducing digital evidence in court still does apply the same basic HARROWing principles found in all evidence codes – whether introducing physical item or digital evidence.

HARROWing my mnemonic to remind us of evidence principles to consider when introducing physical pieces of evidence, especially ones with words on or in them. HARROWing - defined as extremely distressing, agonizing, excruciating, torturing, painful, and causing physical or psychological pain – is how many new lawyers describe their experience trying to introduce evidence

H = Hearsay;
A= Authentication;
R= R401 relevancy (sometime called "logical relevancy);
R=R403 (sometimes called "legal Relevancy);
OW = Original Writings (traditionally known as Best Evidence).

The same rules of evidence apply to ESI as they do to paper and physical evidence. The most challenging foundational issues for digital evidence are establishing:1) who created the digital evidence (the author), and 2) has it been altered?

A Variety of Standards
Different standards have developed in various jurisdictions for authenticating digital evidence.

The Texas courts, and probably most jurisdictions, use an authentication standard identical to the standard used for traditional forms of evidence – "evidence sufficient to support a finding (R 901). The Texas standard can be thought of and remembered by the state's placement on a map – it is a lower standard.

However, the Maryland courts, and a few others, have developed a higher standard – like Maryland's placement on a map. Maryland courts seem to require that the proponent of digital evidence prove that the digital evidence has not been altered or hacked, it comes from a certain source, and that no one other than the owner could have used the electronic device to send or post the message. This view of EIS authentication is concerned about "voodoo information taken from the Internet." It creates a standard that can seldom be met. However, in more recent cases Maryland courts have backed away from that high standard and seem now to favor a more traditional approach for authenticating digital evidence.

The Grimm, Joseph & Capra article, Best Practices for Authenticating Digital Evidence 69 Baylor L.R. 1 (2017) is a great source for understanding factors in authenticating digital evidence. That article presents an overview of how Rules of Evidence 104(a) and 104(b) interact in the authentication process and argues that digital evidence should be authenticated requiring only evidence

"sufficient to support a finding," - which is a low standard.

The authors offer the opinion that,

"Generally speaking, it will be a rare case in which an item of digital evidence cannot be authenticated."

The article covers various ways to authenticate digital evidence. Most helpful will be the examples of various types of circumstantial evidence that would qualify as "distinctive characteristics" under R901(b)(4). Additional, less frequently used methods of authenticating evidence are also covered, such as, personal knowledge of a witness, business records (in some email situations), jury comparison, and production in discovery.

Distinctive Characteristics and Circumstantial Evidence Used to Authenticate Emails and Text Messages as having been sent by a particular person or as having been received by a particular person

There are many possible ways to use circumstantial evidence to qualify as "distinctive characteristics" to authenticate Electronically Stored Information (ESI) under R901(b)(4) Distinctive Characteristics and the Like. Appearance, contents, substance, internal patterns, or other distinctive characteristics of the item taken together with all the circumstances are almost endless.

The Grimm, Joseph & Capra article offers many extremely valuable suggestions about circumstantial evidence which can be considered "distinctive characteristics" and used to authenticate digital evidence under R901(b)(4).

For example, when laying the foundation for an email or text, consider:
    1) information in or about the email or text
    2) information outside the email or text itself that leads back to the author
    3) forensic information, and
    4) information outside the email or text itself indicating receipt of the message.

Factors suggested by Grimm, Joseph, and Capra used to authenticate authorship or receipt of a message include:

    1) information in or about the email or text, such as:
        - the email address, email signature, a nickname, a screen name, initials, a moniker, the author's customary use of emoji or emoticons, a writing style (including phrases and abbreviations frequently used by the author), referring to facts only the author or small group of people would know about, facts uniquely tied to the author, information about the author's family, photos of the author, items of importance to the author such as a car or a pet, and other such information

2) information outside the email or text itself that leads back to the author, such as:
- the email was part of a chain or series of emails from the same person, the claimed author told the witness to expect an email from the author, the author orally repeats its content soon after the email is sent, the author discusses the contents of the email with the third party, the author leaves a voicemail substantially of the same content, and other such information

3) forensic information, such as:
- an email's hash values or testimony from a forensic witness that the email came from a particular device at a particular time, and other such information

4) information outside the email or text itself indicating receipt of the message, such as:
- a reply was received by the sender that came from the recipient, later conduct of the recipient reflects knowledge of the contents of the sent message, later communication of the recipient reflects knowledge of the message, and the message was received and accessed on an electronic device in the possession of the recipient, and other such information.

Presenting the Digital Evidence from a Cell Phone in Court

- Print the page from the phone and use the printout in court.
- If a photo comes from a cell phone, attach the picture to an email, and then print from a computer.
- Screenshot the information (picture, text message, email, social media post), email it, then print from a computer.

Self-Authentication for Digital Evidence

Recent amendments to the Federal Rules of Evidence (and the <u>Ohio Rules of Evidence</u>) allow for self-authentication of certified records
– See FRE 902(13)&(14); ORE 902)13&(14)

Digital Evidence and Self-Authentication

FRE 902(13) (Added to FRE Dec. 2017)
(13) Certified Records Generated by an Electronic Process or System. A record generated by an electronic process or system that produces an accurate result, as shown by a certification of a qualified person that complies with the certification requirements of Rule 902(11) or (12). The proponent must also meet the notice requirements of Rule 902(11).
 [JB: covers text messages, cell phone photos, GPS data, and other ESI]

> **Note: Ohio has adopted this rule.**
> 13 states have this rule: Alabama, Arizona, Illinois, Iowa, Maryland, Mississippi, Nebraska, New Hampshire, North Dakota, Ohio, Pennsylvania, Utah, and Wyoming.

FRE 902(14) Certified Data Copied from an Electronic Device, Storage Medium, or File. Data copied from an electronic device, storage medium, or file, if authenticated by a process of digital identification, as shown by a certification of a qualified person that complies with the certification requirements of Rule 902(11) or (12). The proponent also must meet the notice requirements of Rule 902(11).

> **Note: Ohio has adopted this rule.**
> 13 states have this rule: Alabama, Arizona, Illinois, Iowa, Maryland, Mississippi, Nebraska, New Hampshire, North Dakota, Ohio, Pennsylvania, Utah, and Wyoming.

Email – Witness is the Sender (Outgoing Email)

Q: How did you notify Cut-Rate about …
A: I sent an email to Dan Jones

Q: What email address did you use?
A: DJones@Cutrate.com

Q: How do you know that was the correct address?
A: He and I have email back and forth for a few months, and all of his emails to me came from that email address

Q: Let me show you what has been marked as plaintiff's proposed exhibit #1.

Q: What is it? (A printout of the email I sent to Jones that day.).

Q: How do you know that? (I wrote it. I remember it. It was in my "sent mail" folder.)

Q: Your Honor I offer the exhibit into evidence.

Email – Witness is the Recipient (Incoming Email)

Do you know Dan Jones?

How do you know him?

Are you familiar with the email address DJones@Cutrate.com?

Have you received emails from Dan Jones in the past?

Have you sent emails to Dan Jones at that address?

Has he responded to your emails from that email address?

Is that email address in your email contacts?

In late April, did you receive an email from Dan Jones about selling liquor?

Did you recognize email address as being from Dan Jones?

I am handing you what has been marked as proposed exhibit #7. You recognize it?

What is it? (A: The email from Dan Jones)

Why would you say that's an email from Dan Jones? [provides information about distinctive characteristics of this email]

How did you get a paper copy of this email? (A: I printed it out.)

Is this a true and accurate printout of that email?

Your Honor, I offer the proposed exhibit into evidence.

> [The email reads: "I might be getting fired. They caught me selling booze to drunks again."]

Text Message
Received by Witness

Do you know Y?

Do you communicate with Y on a regular basis?

In what ways to you communicate with Y?

Did you receive a text message from the Y [recently; on or about _ date, on the topic of ..., etc.]?

Would you recognize a printout of the message if you were to see it again?

Let me show you what has been marked as proposed exhibit # 1. Do you recognize it?

What is it? [Ans: A screenshot from my cell phone]

How do you know that this is a message from Y? [It is similar to other messages I have received from Y in that ...]

How did it appear when it arrived on your phone? [Showed up under the name and with the picture I had previously assigned to Y]

What other distinctive characteristics did you notice about the message? [provide as many as distinctive characteristics possible]

Is it a fair and accurate representation of the text message you received [recently; on or about _ date, on the topic of visiting your son, etc.]?

Has it been altered in any way?

I would like to enter the proposed exhibit into evidence

Social Media
Facebook, Instagram, Snapchat, Twitter, and other Posts

Do you know B?

How long have you known him?

Are you familiar with Facebook?

Does B have a Facebook account?

Have you seen posts by B on his Facebook account in the past?

How do you know that B made those posts? [provide distinctive characteristics]

Have you seen a posting on B's Facebook account about [the matter in question]?

Let the record reflect that I am handing you what has been marked as proposed exhibit 12 and ask if you can identify it?

What is it?

Is that a screenshot of the Facebook posting by B about ___?

What day did you take the screenshot?

Is it a true and accurate screenshot of that posting?

Is the post still on B's account? [Ask this question only if it is currently on the account.]

I offer the proposed exhibit into evidence.

Internet Website – Web Posting

Did you visit Professor John Barkai's webpage? [Yes]

How did you access it? [Googled "John Barkai" on my phone]

How did you find his page?
   Ans: I clicked on the link that said "Prof. John Barkai Homepage."

What did you find when you clicked on that link for the homepage?
   Ans: I found his list of courses and other posts.

Did you click on any particular link?
   Ans: I clicked Hawaii Rules of Evidence (HRE) Book Page

What did you find on that page when you clicked on it?
   A: I found a link to buy from Amazon a copy of this Rules of Evidence Handbook.

Let me show you what's been marked as proposed exhibit # 14. Can you identify it?
   A: Yes. It's a screenshot of that webpage with instructions about how to buy a copy of this book from Amazon.

Was that screenshot a print of the page from his website?
   A: Yes, I printed it myself.

Is this exhibit a fair and accurate copy of that webpage? [Yes]

Has this exhibit of the screenshot been altered or otherwise change from the image on your phone in any way? [No]

I offer the exhibit into evidence.

Fax – Incoming

Does your office have a fax machine?

Do you send outgoing faxes?

Do you receive incoming faxes?

Have you received purchase orders from the defendant by fax in the past?

Let me show you plaintiff's proposed exhibit # 27 and ask if you can identify it? [A: Yes. I can]

What is it? [A: A fax I received about six months ago from the defendant]

Why do you say this fax came from the defendant?
A: There are number of factors in addition to the document being written on the defendant's letterhead stationery. The fax is signed by the head of defendant's purchasing department, and I am familiar with her signature from our past dealings. Further, imprinted on the bottom of this fax sheet is the fax number for the defendant's company, and I have faxed prior documents to the defendant by using that number. Finally, the document relates to the purchase of some equipment that I had discussed with the defendant's head of purchasing just a few hours before the fax arrived at my office.

Is this document in the same or substantially the same condition as it was when you received it? [A: Yes, it is exactly the same.]

There have been no alterations or changes? [A: None whatsoever.]

Your Honor, I move that this proposed exhibit be admitted into evidence.

Laying Foundations

Expert Opinions

> **Ohio uses the Daubert standard.**
> See, Ohio Rule of Evidence 702

> **Admissibility of Expert Testimony.**
> The majority of states have explicitly adopted the Daubert (FRE702) standard. A minority of states use either the Frye ("general acceptance") standard or some combination of Daubert and Frye standards.
> Additionally, "general acceptance" is part of the Daubert standard.

Four Part Expert Opinion Foundation and Testimony

> 1. Elicit the <u>background and qualifications</u> of the expert
> 2. Tender or offer the witness as expert in a particular field
>   (e.g., 'general medicine.")
>   – Opponent is allowed to voir dire (test qualifications by cross examination limited to the expert's qualifications, but not the facts of this case)
> 3. <u>Offer the expert's opinion</u> or conclusion (to a particular standard such as "reasonable medical certainty") FRE 702
> 4. <u>Offer the basis for opinion</u> FRE703
>   – Including reasonable reliance on inadmissible evidence
>   – Disclosure of inadmissible evidence?

Three Simple Questions

> 1) Q: "Do you have an opinion as to whether…
> 2) Q: "What is that opinion?"
> 3) Q: "How did you reach that opinion?
>   A: [including inadmissible information reasonably relied upon by experts in the particular field, FRE 703]

How to Start
The expert witness examination normally starts with questions to establish the witness' qualifications to testify as an expert.

Topics for Background and Qualifications of an Expert:
- formal education, work experience, number of previous times retained, qualified, and testified as an expert, in which courts, on-the-job training, non-degree training courses, publications in the field, teaching in the field, memberships in related professional associations, and any other topics relevant to showing the person is an expert.

Tender / Offer

After presenting the expert's background and qualifications, in jurisdictions where the judge must "certify" or "find" that the witness is an expert and is to permitted to testify as an expert, the lawyer presenting the expert then "tenders" or "offers" the witness to the judge as an expert, stating the field of expertise.

"I offer/tender Mr. X as an expert in the field of..."

"I ask the court to certify Ms. Y as an expert in the field of ..."

Can you call the expert an "expert?"

After any voir dire (a limited cross examination to test the qualifications of the witness) by opposing counsel and objections, the judge rules on whether the expert can continue to testify as an expert. Some courts do not allow the lawyer to use the word "expert" to refer to the expert witness. but the judge is still changed with the responsibility of determining if the witness is qualified as an expert. Yet no one uses the word "expert" in front of lay fact finders. The apparent reason for such a practice is, as explained below.

The 2000 Advisory Committee Notes to the amendment to Federal Rule of Evidence 702 says, in part:

> "...The use of the term "expert" in the Rule does not, however, mean that a jury should actually be informed that a qualified witness is testifying as an "expert." Indeed, there is much to be said for a practice that prohibits the use of the term "expert" by both the parties and the court at trial. Such a practice "ensures that trial courts do not inadvertently put their stamp of authority" on a witness's opinion, and protects against the jury's being "overwhelmed by the so-called 'experts'."

More Tenders/Offers of the expert

"We believe that Mr. Taylor <u>should be permitted</u> to offer his opinions in this case."

"I <u>tender</u> Dr. Barron as an expert in the field of family medicine and request that she be allowed to testify as such.

"I <u>offer</u> Dr. Rosenberg as an expert in the field of neurology."

"Judge, we ask that the court <u>accept</u> Dr. Shigeta as an expert in civil engineering."

Offering the Opinion

Traditionally, the opinion is delivered in a two questions sequence:
Q1: Do you have an opinion as ….?
A: Yes
Q2: What is that opinion?

"Do you have an opinion, <u>within a reasonable degree of scientific certainty</u>, as to the time of death of Ms. X?"

"Do you have an opinion, <u>to a reasonable degree of medical probability</u>, as to whether the motorcycle accident caused Mr. Fulbright's epilepsy?"

"Do you have an opinion, <u>to a reasonable degree of engineering certainty</u>, as to whether the XXX caused the bridge to fail?"

"Do you have an opinion whether Mr. X suffered a brain damage as a result of the fight?"

Standards for Stating an Expert's Opinion
There are no minimum standards under R702 describing how "good" an expert's opinion must be to be stated in court. By case law, some courts and jurisdictions require that the standard must be stated to a
  "reasonable degree of [medical] <u>certainty</u>," or a
  "reasonable degree of [scientific] <u>probability</u>."
Other jurisdictions simply allow an expert to state an opinion without any specific qualification.
  "What did your examination reveal?"

The above standards of "certainty" and "probability" are vague and rather unhelpful standards to a lay jury or courts-martial member who might be able to understand percentages, but who is given no guidance to the certainty or probability. Do those standards mean 51%, 65%, 75%, 85%, 95%, etc.? "Preponderance of the evidence" does have an associated percentage (50%+), but terms such as "sufficient to support a finding," "clear and convincing," "beyond a reasonable doubt," as well as "certainty" and "probability" do not. Simply, use whatever standard your judge and jurisdiction require.

In an attempt to be persuasive, some lawyers ask the experts questions like:

"How positive are you of your opinion?"
"What is the degree of your certainty?"

Inadmissible Information Reasonably Relied Upon

In the federal courts and a majority of the states, experts can base their opinions on hearsay and other inadmissible evidence. Federal Rule of Evidence says in part:

"If experts in the particular field would reasonably rely on those kinds of facts or data in forming an opinion on the subject, they need not be admissible for the opinion to be admitted."

You should have in your tool chest of questions this question.
"Is that the type of information reasonably relied upon by experts in your field?

Remember

Whoever has the Biggest, Most Qualified Expert Might Win

Because opposing parties often have opposing experts, who have reached opposing conclusions, the advocacy principle is for you to try to present a more qualified and more credible expert than your opponent's expert. If "your" expert's testimony and conclusions are believed on the issue that the experts are testifying about, you are more likely to win your case.

History and Restyling of the Federal Rules of Evidence

The Ohio Rules of Evidence are based upon, and in many parts very similar to, the Federal Rules of Evidence (FRE), which were adopted in 1975 and have been amended many times over the years. Approximately 46 states have adopted evidence codes, by statute or court rule, which are patterned on the FRE. The states without FRE based evidence codes are California, Kansas, Missouri, and New York. The California Evidence Code, which was the first state evidence code, took effect in 1965 and is quite different in structure than any other state evidence code.

Although most states modeled their evidence rules after the FRE, almost every state has some evidence provisions which are different from the federal rules and some states have very significant differences.

The FRE were "restyled" in 2011 to
> "make them more easily understood and to make style and terminology consistent throughout the rules. These changes are intended to be stylistic only. There is no intent to change any result in any ruling on evidence admissibility.... The [Restyling] Committee made special efforts to reject any purposed style improvement that might result in a substantive change in the application of a rule." --- See Restyled Rules Committee Note for Restyled Rules of Evidence.

At least sixteen (16) states, have restyled their rules of evidence: Arizona (2012), Delaware (2017), Idaho (2018), Indiana (2013), Iowa (2017), Maine (2015), Michigan (2024), Mississippi (2016), New Hampshire (2017), New Mexico (2012), North Dakota (2014), Pennsylvania (2013), South Dakota (2016), Texas (2014), Utah (2012), and West Virginia (2014). The Military (2013) and the Commonwealth of the Northern Mariana Islands (2015) have also restyled.

Teaching Evidence Since 4 B.C.

Art by Dan Mazanec

John Barkai has been teaching evidence since 4 B.C. – that is 4 years "Before Computers" were used at the University of Hawaii Law School. His major criminal trial practice experience was in 1972-1973 in Detroit, and included jury trials on charges for Felony Murder, Criminal Sexual Conduct (Statutory Rape in 1973), Armed Robbery, Assault, and CCW (Carrying A Concealed Weapon). He did not use the federal rules of evidence at that time. No one did. The Federal Rules did not go into effect until July 1975, by which time he was a fulltime law professor. For the past 50 years, he has taught a criminal clinic in which his students try traffic and misdemeanor cases under the state student practice rule.

Books by John Barkai

The Pocket Guide to Common Trial Objections & Evidentiary Foundations

Federal Rules of Evidence Handbook with Common Objections & Evidentiary Foundations

Military Rules of Evidence Handbook with Common Objections & Evidentiary Foundations

Negotiation and Mediation Communication Gambits for Breaking Impasses and More: What Do I Say When I Want To …

Humor in Trial Evidence: Cartoon Caption Contest Winners and Challenges from My Evidence Class

Humor in Negotiations & ADR: Cartoon Caption Contest Winners from the ABA Dispute Resolution Magazine

The following evidence books in my
Handbooks with Common Objections & Evidentiary Foundations series

Alabama	Illinois	Nebraska	Rhode Island
Alaska	Indiana	Nevada	South Carolina
Arizona	Iowa	New Hampshire	South Dakota
Arkansas	Kentucky	New Jersey	Tennessee
California **	Louisiana	New Mexico	Texas **
Colorado	Maine **	North Carolina	Utah
Connecticut	Maryland	North Dakota	Vermont
Delaware	Massachusetts	Ohio	Virginia
Florida **	Michigan **	Oklahoma	Washington
Georgia	Minnesota	Oregon	West Virginia
Hawaii	Mississippi	Pennsylvania **	Wisconsin
Idaho	Montana		Wyoming

** Also published "Just the Rules" books for these states.

Massachusetts, Missouri, and New York do not have rules of evidence, but Massachusetts and New York have published "Guides" to evidence.

Handbooks for U.S. affiliated jurisdictions.

American Samoa	Marshall Islands
Chuuk	Northern Mariana Islands
Federated States of Micronesia	Palau
Guam	Pohnpei
Kosrae	Yap
Puerto Rico	U.S. Virgin Islands

The following international evidence books in my
Handbooks with Common Objections & Evidentiary Foundations series

Antigua and Barbuda **	Kiribati**
Australia	Korea **
New South Wales **	Malaysia **
Queensland**	Nauru
South Australia**	New Zealand **
Tasmania**	Nigeria **
Victoria **	Papua New Guinea **
Western Australia**	People's Republic of China **
Bangladesh **	Philippines **
Bhutan **	Republic of China (Taiwan) **
Canada **	Singapore **
Alberta **	Sir Lanka **
British Columbia **	Samoa **
Manitoba **	Sierra Leone **
Ontario **	Solomon Islands **
Saskatchewan **	South Africa **
Cook Islands **	Tanzania **
Cyprus **	Tokelau **
Fiji	Tonga **
Hong Kong **	UK (United Kingdom) **
India **	Zimbabwe **
Jamica**	

** Also Published "Just the Rules" or
"Just the Evidence Acts/Ordinances" for the above jurisdictions

To find John Barkai's evidence and cartoon books
1. Go to the Amazon website – www.Amazon.com
2. Enter into the search bar: - John Barkai
3. For a particular state or country, enter into the Amazon search bar
     - John Barkai [state/country name]

Dedication

To my wife Linda and my adult twin daughters Hope and Leah,
who bring me so much joy and enrich my life
and
to the hundreds of my former evidence and clinical students
who learned these rules of evidence with me
over the past 50 plus years
at the William S. Richardson School of Law
at the University of Hawaii
and
Wayne State Law School in Detroit.

About the Author

Professor Barkai is a former Detroit Michigan criminal trial lawyer, a fulltime law professor for more than 50 years - a Professor of Law at the William S. Richardson School of Law at the University of Hawaii for 45 years and taught at Wayne State University for 5 years. He has taught evidence since 1981 and has been the Director, and now Co-Director, of the Law School's Clinical Program since 1978. He has been a member of the Hawaii Supreme Court's Standing Committee on the Rules of Evidence since 1993. He has a BBA MBA, and JD, all from the University of Michigan. For the past 50 years, he has taught a criminal clinic in which his students try traffic and minor criminal cases under the state student practice rule.

This book, and his many other evidence handbooks, were inspired by handbooks he created in 2019 for a workshop for Pacific Island Judges from American Samoa, Marshall Islands, Federated States of Micronesia, Chuuk, Kosrae, Pohnpei, and Yap.

He has published over 160 evidence books for all 50 U.S. states, territories, and affiliated jurisdictions, the federal and military rules of evidence, Asian, South Asian, Pacific Island, African countries, Australian states, Canadian provinces, and the United Kingdom. He also has evidence and negotiation & ADR cartoon captioning books on Amazon as well as a book on effective communication for negotiation and mediation.

Since summer 2025 has been actively engaged in creating BarkaiBots, online AI bots (chatbots) which are practice partners designed to help lawyers, judges, and students learn to better perform trial advocacy, negotiation, and mediation skills.

BarkaiBots: 24/7 Oral Practice Tools for Trial Advocacy

This book includes free access to **BarkaiBots**—interactive AI courtroom simulations that function both as responsive practice partners and built-in personal coaches to help users improve their advocacy. Using a free ChatGPT account on a desktop, laptop, phone, or tablet, lawyers and law students can rehearse advocacy skills 24/7 by conducting realistic simulations with AI witnesses, judges, and opposing counsel.

Practice with a responsive partner. Improve with a built-in coach.

During practice, BarkaiBots respond in real time like courtroom participants; after the exercise, they provide coaching feedback to help users refine their advocacy. These simulations allow users to practice core courtroom skills, including conducting direct and cross-examinations, handling evasive witnesses, making and responding to objections, laying evidentiary foundations, conducting impeachment, presenting openings and closings, arguing motions, and even running full mock trials. Users can also customize a BarkaiBot by uploading a short hypothetical fact pattern, allowing practice with scenarios drawn from their own cases while avoiding disclosure of confidential client information. BarkaiBots allow advocates to rehearse, receive coaching, and refine their advocacy before stepping into the courtroom.

How to pronounce BarkaiBots
My family name is pronounced – Bar-key.

WHY BARKAIBOTS ARE DIFFERENT
• **Practice with a responsive partner—not a mirror.**
BarkaiBots respond like live participants in a courtroom, allowing users to question witnesses, respond to objections, and adapt to answers in real time.
• **Immediate coaching and feedback**
After a practice session, BarkaiBots provide detailed feedback and coaching that can be adjusted to different levels of guidance.
• **Unlimited rehearsal opportunities**
Users can repeat exercises as often as they wish, refining their advocacy through practice, feedback, and improvement.
• **Self-review of courtroom delivery**
Sessions can be run in a private Zoom meeting so users can record and review their performance, listening to their questioning style, observing posture, tone, and other nonverbal aspects of advocacy.

How BarkaiBots Work
BarkaiBots are AI-powered conversational practice partners.
You speak (or type), and the bot responds in role. It can act as a witness, opposing counsel, judge, or even prospective jurors for voir dire practice.

The learning method is simple and powerful:
You perform.
The bot reacts.
You request feedback.
You repeat.

Access the Amazon BarkaiBots Start Page
on your computer
by typing the internet address below into your internet browser

https://bit.ly/ABBSP

(ABBSP = Amazon BarkaiBots Start Page)
or
Access the Amazon BarkaiBots Start Page
on your phone
by using your phone's camera to open the QR below

Scan with your phone's camera

Either method takes you to the "Amazon BarkaiBots Start Page," which contains:
- A current list of available BarkaiBots with direct links to each bot
- A quick start guide
- A link to the Amazon BarkaiBots Folder with additional materials, including simulation facts

BarkaiBot Access and Technical Notes
- Access does not require purchase of this book.
- It does require a free online account on the hosting platform (https://chatgpt.com) Click "Sign Up."
- No credit card is required for a basic account.
- Verify your email and complete the registration.
- Return to the BarkaiBots page and open any bot.

Features such as voice capability, session length, and interface layout may vary depending on:
- Device (desktop, laptop, phone, tablet)
- Web browser v. mobile app
- Free v. paid account
- Platform updates

If voice mode is unavailable, you may type your questions and answers. However, BarkaiBots were designed for oral practice. I use ChatGPT Plus ($20/month) on a desktop to build and test my bots. Your experience may vary depending on your setup.

Why I Created BarkaiBots
With more than 50 years as a full-time law professor teaching evidence, clinics, simulations, and externships, I have seen firsthand that students and lawyers can find a great deal of information about litigation skills, but seldom get to perform those skills and almost never receive structured feedback. Trial work is an oral performance. A law school evidence class does not prepare students to apply the rules dynamically in a courtroom, and lawyers in practice get very limited opportunities to refine their trial skills and virtually never get extensive, structured coaching.

Effective advocacy requires:
- Timing
- Question sequencing
- Witness control
- Responsiveness to new information
- Judgment under pressure
- Practical application of evidence rules

Those skills improve most when practiced aloud and repetitively.

BarkaiBots provide a safe place to practice:
- Without embarrassment
- Without opposing counsel present
- Without client pressure
- Without scheduling constraints

Since 2018, I have published over 160 evidence and dispute resolution books covering all U.S. jurisdictions and many international ones. Some of those books, including this one, include sample transcripts that can be read aloud to practice foundations and impeachment. Experience has taught me that transcripts alone are not enough. Students can follow a script and still struggle when the facts change. They can memorize phrasing without developing sequencing judgment. What was missing was a way to practice decision-making in real time.

In mid-2025, I began creating custom AI ChatGPT bots for my litigation and dispute resolution courses. Those bots became structured practice partners for my students and provided them with immediate feedback and coaching 24/7.

Gamechanger!

Now I am sharing selected BarkaiBots with my Amazon readers

Professional Responsibility and Confidentiality
I do not have access to, or control over, what users say or upload when using BarkaiBots.

Never upload confidential client information to any AI platform.

You remain responsible under the applicable
rules of professional conduct
for protecting client confidentiality.

What BarkaiBots are not designed to:
- Conduct legal research
- Analyze appellate decisions
- Draft memoranda or briefs
- Generate case citations

BarkaiBots are rehearsal tools — not research tools. AI systems can make mistakes. So can lawyers. Always exercise independent professional judgment.

Final Thoughts
BarkaiBots are offered in the spirit of helping lawyers and students gain confidence through practice. Advocacy is variable and subjective. Every lawyer develops a personal style. The suggestions and feedback you receive from a BarkaiBot come from general advocacy principles and programmed training structures — not from a live review of your specific performance by Professor Barkai.

If you use skills developed through BarkaiBots in court, what you say and do remains your responsibility. The voice in the courtroom is yours.

I wish you success in the practice of law or your law school courses if you are still a student.

John Barkai

www.ingramcontent.com/pod-product-compliance
Lightning Source LLC
Chambersburg PA
CBHW071411210526
45465CB00001B/343